ENTREPRENEURSHIP AND WOMEN EMPOWERMENT

Edited by

Dr. K. Padmasree Jalandhar

Associate Professor & Head
Department of Commerce
School of Business Studies
Central University of Karnataka
Gulbarga Karnataka
(India)

DPH

DISCOVERY PUBLISHING HOUSE PVT. LTD.
NEW DELHI-110 002

Published by:
Tilak Wasan
DISCOVERY PUBLISHING HOUSE PVT. LTD.
4383/4B, Ansari Road, Darya Ganj
New Delhi-110 002 (India)
Phone : +91-11-23279245, 43596064-65
Fax : +91-11-23253475
E-mail : discoverypublishinghouse@gmail.com
sales@discoverypublishinggroup.com
parul.wasan@gmail.com
web : www.discoverypublishinggroup.com

***First Edition:* 2014**

ISBN: 978-93-5056-416-5

Entrepreneurship and Women Empowerment

Printed at:
Dynamic Printers
Delhi

Preface

"She plays many roles, yet she is never on the main stage; she may have dreams and visions, But her realization often different. She aspires to make a difference, But all there is indifference. Open your eyes to her..... (certainly she will make difference)"...

In India half of the population constitutes women hence Rapid Economic development of the country depends on women empowerment. Hence there is a dire need of empowering women for the economic development of the country. Being women entrepreneurship one of the catalysts, has a pivotal role in attainment of women empowerment. Though essential efforts were initiated.by the Government and other agencies nationally and Internationally to strengthen women entrepreneurs the number of women entrepreneurs are increasing over the years in absolute terms but not in real terms. Anticipated results could not result in increasing women entrepreneurs in India, and could not reach the women in rural and backward areas due to various constraints like socio-cultural barriers, security risks, motivational factors, lack of awareness about opportunities, financial assistance etc., hence the present seminar intended to focus on the importance of entrepreneurship as one of the catalyst for women empowerment by deliberate discussions made by the eminent speakers and academic discussions, case studies on different themes like problems and prospects of women entrepreneurs, role of government and other agencies, financial institutions, educational institutions, present positions of entrepreneurs in the current century in particular and women empowerment in general.

Good number of research papers received on focused themes from various sections across the nation among them a few are from interdisciplinary streams *viz.*, History, English, Bio-technology, Engineering, Education etc. These papers have been classified on the basis of different themes of the present seminar and the sessions are also planned accordingly chaired and co-chaired by eminent professors. The selected papers are presented in the present volume.

The seminar was successful with the financial support received from Andhra Pradesh State council of Higher education, Hyderabad, and from local sources from successful entrepreneurs, and educational institutions *viz.,* G. Sesha Reddy, Mani Group of Industires, Kadapa, Sri. Gangi Reddy, S.V. Degree College, Kadapa, Sri. Rama Moorthy, Chaitanya Chemicals, Kadapa, Sri. K. Siva Nanda Reddy, Kandula Group of Institutions, Kadapa, Sri. Nazeer Ahmad, Bharat College of Engineering and Technology for Women, Kadapa, Sri. Khasim Khan, Vidya Sadhana Group of Colleges, Kadapa, Sri. G. Subba Reddu, Srihari Degree College, Kadapa, Sri. S. Hari Kishore Reddy, Kishore paper converters, Kadapa, Sri. Nityananda Reddy, Sri. Gopal Swamy, Saraswathi degree College, Kadapa, and Saraswathi Degree College. I take this opportunity to thank them profusely.

Dr. K. Padmasree Jalandhar

Acknowledgements

I am very much thankful to all the paper contributors of this book.

I express my special thanks to my hubby Mr. Anchula Siva Jalandharachari, my Son Mast. Anchula Siva Datta Sai, Daughter Miss. A. Yogyasree Rakshita, My Mother-in-law and Father-in-law Smt. A. Laxmi Prasad, and Late Sri. A. Veerabrahma Chari, My mother and fataher Smt. K. Govindamma and Sri Late. K. Agasthappachari, and family members Mast. Kundan Sree Vallab, Kum. Leena Sreevalli, Dr. A. Bharathi Devi, Mr. Brahmam, A. Yugandharachari, Smt. Anuradha Yugandhar, A. Viswarupachari, and Smt. Lakshmi Viswarupachari for their inspiration and cooperation with out which I could not complete this assignment.

I express my sincere thanks to Mr. Tilak Wasan for bringing out this edited volume.

Contents

1

Women Empowerment through Entrepreneurship
Some Pragmatic Studies

Prof. C. Sivarami Reddy*
Prof. P. Mohan Reddy**
Dr. P. Saritha***

ABSTRACT

Entrepreneurship amongst women has been a recent development. The entrepreneur is a person who has enterprising quality, takes initiative and establishes an economic activity or enterprise. The entrepreneur means to 'undertake', i.e., the person who undertakes the risk of new enterprise. Starting and operating an enterprise involves considerable risk and effort on the part of the entrepreneurs particularly in the light of high failure rate. The status of women is in vogue in many countries even today, though in a lesser scale. Moreover, the position a woman enjoys varies from country to country according to the prevailing conditions and socio-cultural environment which prevails. It is true that age-old practices cannot be eradicated overnight. So the need of the hour is women empowerment

* Registrar, Yogi Vemana University, Kadapa - 3 and Professor, Department of Commerce, S.V., University, Tirupati - 517 502, A.P.

** Professor, Department of Commerce, S.V., University, Tirupati - 517 502, A.P.

*** Assistant Professor, Department of Business Administration, Yogi Vemana University, Kadapa - 3, A.P.

both through provision of employment and enterprise creation. The former leads to endogenous empowerment and the latter gives rise to exogenous empowerment. The enterprises started by women are so greatly influenced by the decisions and desires of the members of the family. Women entrepreneurs who receive support from family, relatives and other support systems could manage their own enterprises successfully. An attempt was made in this study to examine the role of family for successful women entrepreneurship. The data was collected from the women entrepreneurs of Kadapa district in A.P. Case-studies were also collected for in-depth analysis. The results of case studies revealed that women need for effective enterprise management, a large quantity of co-operation and encouragement in the sphere of activity, at all levels in home, in society and from governmental organizations. The study reveals that women are trying to exercise variety of business ideas, but needed support from the family members and positive attitude from society, in particular for establishing and sustaining in their enterprises. Encouragement by the family is the most important factor facilitating entrepreneurship in spite of strong will and firm determination, women entrepreneurs look for support from family members, friends, government and from others in the immediate society.

ABOUT THE TOPIC

Family is the foundation of social life, it forms the nucleus of the social structure. An individual is born, brought up and attains a distinct personality in the environs of the family. It is this institution which preserves, protects and develops the human race. A family is a group of persons united by the ties of marriage, blood or adoption, constituting a single household interacting and intercommunicating with each other in their respective social role of husband and wife, mother and father, son and daughter, brother and sister and creating and containing a common culture. Women are working to earn livelihood along with men since times immemorial, their contribution in monetary term remain unaccounted or if at all accounted it is given very low value. It doesn't mean that women do not possess the capacity. In fact women even the illiterate rural ones practice and use all the tools and techniques of efficient management like financial management, human resource management, time and space management and maintenance management.

ROLE OF WOMEN IN SOCIETY

A woman has diversified functions to perform in the family as user, conserver, protector and creator/promoter of resources. Only thing is they do not use the modern jargons coined by the experts. Gone are the days when a man could boast of being capable of feeding the whole family. Now the woman must supplement it through whatever skill she has acquired. Now the women are playing multidisciplinary roles (Fig. 1.1).

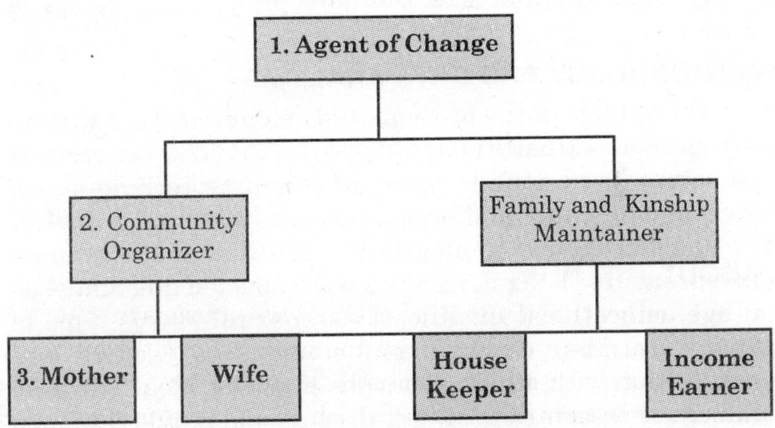

Fig. 1.1: Multiple Roles of Women

1. Less known, completely ignored.
2. Known, less explored.
3. Well known, well explored.

In the process of conceptualizing the term entrepreneur, it is noted that though it is originated in the west, it has undergone many changes from time to time. Woman entrepreneur is an individual who takes up a challenging role in which she constantly interacts and adjusts herself with social, resource and support spheres in a society. By enabling women to become entrepreneurs and to participate fully and more effectively in a wide range of economic and especially industrial activities, they improve their position and also make greater progress towards higher economic growth, improved productivity, improved distribution of income, reduction in poverty and unemployment. A vital interface exists between family and women entrepreneurs. The quality of women entrepreneurship is essentially influenced by the family and its immediate environment. The culture in which they are born and reared makes them depend on family members, friends and neighbours for decision-making in issues related to day-to-day living. The family support influences the entrepreneurial success of women.

METHODOLOGY AND DATA ANALYSIS

The sample of the present study comprised 150 women entrepreneurs from Kadapa district, A.P. The selection of the sample was done by random sampling technique. An Interview schedule and oral interviews are used to collect the socio-economic demographic profiles of the women entrepreneurs. The information was collected and analysed on age, educational qualifications, marital status, type of family, number of children, motivating factors and consultation with others about the business idea. Two case studies are presented to project the personal profile of women entrepreneurs and for in-depth analysis.

Age Status

Age is an important factor in determining the women entrepreneurship. Hence, the composition of age of women entrepreneurs is selected for the study and which is provided in Table 1.1.

Table 1.1: Age-wise classification of select women entrepreneurs

Age	No. of Respondents	% of Respondents
16-25	20	13
26-35	49	33
36 and Above	81	54
Total	**150**	**100**

Most of the women entrepreneurs (54%) belonged to the age-group of 36 and above and 13 and 33 per cent belonged to the age-group of 16-25 years and 26-35 years respectively. It appears generally women think of a business idea in their thirties. But by that time normally they would have settled in life and have more leisure as their children will be in the school. One more reason for this category turning to entrepreneurship could be that they viewed business is flexible and felt sure that they could manage both house and business easily. Hence, generally the women enter into business after thirties.

Educational Qualifications

Education is one of the inputs for entrepreneurship. It enables the entrepreneur to gather information from different sources and helps them to analyse properly and think innovatively to start the business. The education levels of the selected women entrepreneurs for the study are furnished in the following Table 1.2.

Table 1.2: Educational qualifications of select women entrepreneurs

Education	No. of Respondents	% of Respondents
Illiterates	30	20
Below SSC	80	53
Up to SSC	18	12
Intermediate	16	11
Graduation	6	4
Total	**150**	**100**

From the above Table 1.2, it is clearly indicated that most of the women entrepreneurs studied less than 10th standard (53%) 20 per cent were illiterates and 12 per cent studied up to S.S.C., and only 15 per cent have better educational qualifications. The data reflects that educational qualifications are not influencing women in seeking entrepreneurship. Women may be totally illiterate but they have their own system of accounting and they do manage their small petty trade *i.e.*, vegetable sellers, fisher women and the like not only in urban areas but also in rural areas.

Marital Status

The marital status of the women has a major influence on the women entrepreneurship. The details of the marital status of select women entrepreneurs in Kadapa district are provided in Table 1.3.

Table 1.3: Marital status of select women entrepreneurs

Marital Status	No. of Respondents	% of Respondents
Married	113	75
Unmarried	37	25
Total	**150**	**100**

Most of the women entrepreneurs (75%) are married and unmarried constitute less percentage compared to them. Further some of the married women would receive help directly or indirectly in running the enterprise. Another reason expressed was that the parents feel the economic independence of unmarried girls through entrepreneurship is a barrier for fixing their marriage.

Number of Children

The number of children possessed by the women is another important factor to start the business and do the business very effectively by the select women entrepreneurs for this study. Table 1.4 depicts the number of children possessed by the select women entrepreneurs in Kadapa district.

Table 1.4: Number of children possessed by select women entrepreneurs

No. of Children	No. of Women Entrepreneurs	% of Respondents
None	29	19
1	18	12
2	55	37
3	30	20
4	11	7
5 and Above	7	5
Total	**150**	**100**

From the Table 1.4 it is clear that 68 per cent of women entrepreneurs have less than two children which include 19 per cent having no children and 32 per cent of the respondents have 3 and more children. Less number of children means less responsibility and more free time which must be important motivating factor for these women to take up entrepreneurship.

Nature of the Family

The nature of the family is most important for women empowerment through entrepreneurship because the major support is given by the family members. The following Table 1.5 depicts the nature of the family of selected women entrepreneurs in Kadapa district.

Table 1.5: Nature of the family of select women entrepreneurs

Nature of Family	No. of Respondents	% of Respondents
Individual	135	90
Joint	15	10
Total	**150**	**100**

About 90 per cent of women entrepreneurs have nuclear/individual families and the remaining 10 per cent have joint families as in the present day society, joint families are few. It is assumed that in joint families, elders do not like their daughters or daughter-in-law to go out and practice non-traditional roles despite the dire economic need. Contrary to this assumption the women entrepreneurs from the joint families are getting adequate support from their families.

Type of Business

The type of businesses of women entrepreneurs were categorize into 3 sectors such as trade, production and service sectors for the study (Table 1.6).

Table 1.6: Type of business carried out by select women entrepreneurs

Type of Business	No. of Respondents	% of Respondents
Trade	72	48
Production	27	18
Service Sector	51	34
Total	**150**	**100**

Nearly half (48%) of the select women entrepreneurs belonged to trade sector, they are included in businesses like purchase and sale of products with little or no processing, like provision stores, fancy stores. Only 18 per cent women were in the production sector which involves businesses like manufacturing of products like food products/processing, textiles, garment making and the like. One third of them (34%) belonged to service sector, which included businesses like STD, beauty parlours, grinding/flour mills etc. From the data it can be concluded that women tend to involve themselves more in enterprises which require less risk taking and low investment.

Motivational Factors

Motivational factors include economic necessity, boredom, family support, livelihood and give good life to children.

Economic Necessity

The most important motivating factor to start the entrepreneurship venture was to supplement their family income. Schwartz expressed that 'economic necessity' was found to be one of the most prime motivations in emerging entrepreneurship. It also reveals that there is definite growing awareness in society and women in particular that if the family has to maintain a reasonable standard of living, women should supplement to family income with whatever skill they have.

Boredom

50 per cent of the women stated that they started business for their livelihood and to provide good life for their children respectively. Few women expressed that they felt bored at home, which prompted them to take up an entrepreneurship.

Family Support

Most of the married women entrepreneurs expressed their business idea first to their husband and got their support. The reasons expressed were forgetting consent and financial support. Women owners were greatly influenced by their husbands and families in making a career choice. Most of the women stated that they need the support (emotional support) of their husbands and families. The husbands often received credit for their wives' small business careers.

Table 1.7: Motivating factors for women entrepreneurship

Motivating Factor	No. of Respondents	% of Respondents
To supplement the family income	114	76
Bored at home	21	14
For livelihood	11	7
To give good life to children	4	3
Total	**150**	**100**

Urge to do Business

On the other hand, most of the women entrepreneurs acted on their own idea in setting up their enterprises, which reflects their independence in decision making, family burden and should be welcomed and encouraged. Some of the select women entrepreneurs stated that, they talked about the idea of starting business venture with their friends and relatives.

IN-DEPTH ANALYSIS OF CASE STUDIES IN KADAPA DISTRICT

An in depth analysis of women entrepreneurs of few cases may further high light that it would be difficult for women to start and sustain with entrepreneurship without the moral support of family members and friends.

Case – 1

Saroja Devi, 42 years old residing at Kadapa town of Andhra Pradesh. Her father was an agriculturist whereas her mother is a housewife and one of her sisters engaged in sarees business. She studied up to Intermediate and married a teacher and she is blessed with two children who stay with her. Saroja Devi is very hard working, intelligent and has good leadership qualities. She maintains good relations with people and has good production and service skills. Even at a very young age, when she was at 6th or 7th standard, when ever she was short of pocket money, she used to prepare different types of hair pins with coloured threads and by selling these hair pins, she made extra money.

After marriage, when she did the bridal make up to her cousin, it is praised by every one and this appreciation motivated her to acquire more skills by doing beautician course. Thus she developed a business idea to open a beauty parlour. Her paternal uncle who is well educated, encouraged her very much not only in the way of convincing her family members but also in providing financial support to start beauty parlour. The main reason which influenced Saroja Devi to start business is to supplement her family income, give good life to her children and above all she had an urge to do business. All these triggered her to exploit her skills and opportunities in the immediate environment. Even though initially her family members including her husband discouraged her but after looking at her interest and enthusiasm, they gave green signal. Satisfied with her success they encouraged her and now they support her by doing almost all household work and looking after the children etc.

Her business hours are from 9.00 a.m. to 9.00 p.m. In this regard, with her own words, "I am very much thankful to my husband and in-laws for their support, otherwise it is almost impossible for me to devote this much time. I am not only the first lady in starting a beauty parlour in Kadapa town, but also a leading beautician earning Rs. 25,000/- p.m.

Noted for her performance, Saroja Devi is honoured by getting the trainees for beautician course under government programme. She feels her decision to start business is wise, since her family responsibilities have been almost completed and she can continue in the business as long as she likes.

Case – 2

B. Lakshmi, 33 years old belongs to Proddutur, Kadapa district of Andhra Pradesh. Her father is running a provision store. She studied up to 6th class. She married to a person 11 years back who engaged in the business of Sofa covers repairs, sales, etc., she belonged to nuclear family and gave birth to two children who are residing with her. Lakshmi has very good interest in business. With her own words, "I like to do business and earn for my satisfaction". Before, her marriage she used to earn her pocket money by weaving and sale of wire baskets to friends, relatives, neighbours and others. She also helped her father in his business apart from helping her mother in all kinds of household work. She is intelligent, hard working and has good human relation skills. In talk with Lakshmi, one can find the entrepreneurial qualities prominent in her. She has a strong desire to do business. After marriage, Lakshmi wanted to start business, but she was discouraged by her husband, in-laws and relatives. Meanwhile, she gave birth to two children and spent her time in looking after children but she continued to take some orders of wire baskets occasionally. At one time, she wanted to continue basket making for sales, but she had difficulties in marketing them. As the children are growing, Lakshmi again felt the desire of starting a business due to increased leisure time. She noticed that there is no petty shop in her locality and also there is demand for such a shop as there is a convent school close to her house, which motivated Lakshmi to start a 'petty shop' which includes mostly the items required for children like chocolates, biscuits, notebooks and also other things of general use like shampoos, match boxes, betel leaves etc.

Surprisingly her grand mother started encouraging her to start business, while her mother discouraged her because Lakshmi's husband didn't like the idea of starting business. She started with her own investment of Rs. 200/-. She felt starting this type of business is risk free and more profitable. As her husband and relatives restricted her from opening a shop she started it in the home in a small shelf, which is generally overlooked by many customers except from few regular customers. She is getting low profits, less demand for the items sold due to low investment and advertisement problems. Despite the lack of support from the family, she is able to venture, which indicated her intense entrepreneurial desire. She does all the domestic work in addition to managing the petty shop. She expressed that without family support "It is very difficult for a woman to start and sustain in business".

In-depth analysis of two cases revealed that Saroja Devi and Lakshmi when expressed the idea of starting a business, they faced lot of resistance from their respective families (Table 1.8). But Saroja Devi could discuss the idea with close relative and received help not only in convincing her family members but also investment for her training and business. But, Lakshmi failed to receive support from her husband which is a major constraint for her to expand her business though she started a business in a small scale. Saroja Devi with her father-in-law's support could give a shape to her business and also underwent training for one year. After six months training she started beauty parlor in a good locality.

But it took nearly 8 years for Lakshmi to start business which clearly indicates lack of support for putting the idea into practice. The family was initially opposed to her entrepreneurship. After seeing the performance of Saroja Devi the family started encouraging her and now she claims total support from the family. She admits that she could achieve more than 150 per cent profit, and become good beautician in Kadapa only with family support, recognizing her expertise. Lakshmi is maintaining the start up 10 per cent profit without any change in the business. She is frustrated as she is unable to explore her entrepreneurial potential due to lack of family and environment support.

Table 1.8: Comparative picture of selected pragmatic cases

Stages of Business	Support from Family	Support from Environment	No. of ment	Profit Workers	(%)
Case – 1					
1. Generation of Business Idea	Total Resistance	Father-in-law	—	—	—
2. During Starting Phase (After 1 ½ years of expressing idea)	Less Resistance	– do –	5000	—	—
3. After 1 year	Encouragement	Family and Public	—	2	100
4. After 2 years	Full Family Support	– do –	Increased	Trainees	150
Case – 2					
1. Before Starting	Total Resistance	Total Resistance	—	—	—
2. During Starting Phase (After 8 years of expressing idea)	Total Resistance	Grand Mother	200	—	—
3. After 1 year	Total Resistance	—	—	—	10
4. After 2 years	Continuous Discouragement	—	—	—	10

PROBLEMS OF WOMEN ENTREPRENEURS

In India, women entrepreneurs generally face a large number of problems. Due to these problems, entrepreneurship development among women has not been satisfactory. These barriers can be as follows:

- Lack of self-confidence,
- Male domination society,
- Low risk bearing capacity,
- Lack of encouragement from family,
- Discrimination in upbringing,
- Role conflict,
- Lack of education,
- Low mobility,
- Problem of access to finance,
- Stiff competition.

FINDINGS AND CONCLUSION

- Generally women think of a business idea in their thirties as they viewed business is flexible and felt sure that they could manage both house and business easily. Hence, generally the women enter into business after thirties.
- Educational qualifications are not influencing women in seeking entrepreneurship. Women may be totally illiterate but they have their own system of accounting and they do manage their small petty trade.
- Most of the women entrepreneurs are married because the parents feel the economic independence of unmarried girls through entrepreneurship is a barrier for fixing their marriage.
- Less number of children (one or two) means less responsibility and more free time which must be important motivating factor for the women to take up entrepreneurship.
- In joint families, elders do not like their daughters or daughter-in-law to go out and practice non-traditional roles despite the dire economic need.

- The women tend to involve themselves more in enterprises which require less risk taking and low investment
- Most of the women entrepreneurs acted on their own idea in setting up their enterprises, which reflects their independence in decision making, family burden and should be welcomed and encouraged.

In psychological terms, entrepreneurship may be described as a creative or innovative response supported by a deep sense of motivation in the environment. The study reveals that women are trying to exercise variety of business ideas, but needed support from the family members and positive attitude from society, in particular for establishing and sustaining in their enterprises. Encouragement by the family is the most important factor facilitating entrepreneurship in spite of strong will and firm determination, women entrepreneurs look for support from family members, friends, government and from others in the immediate society.

REFERENCES

DRDA Annual Reports.

Khanka, S.S., 'Entrepreneurial Development', S. Chand and Company Ltd., New Delhi, 2001.

Vasant Desai, 'Dynamics of Entrepreneurial Development and Management', Himalaya Publishing House, Mumbai, 2005.

http://www.gemconsortium.org/download/1232428620182/GEM_Global_08.pdf

http://www.fiwe.org/index.php?option=com_frontpage&Itemid=137

http://awakeindia.org.in/main.php

http://www.census.gov/

www.statebankofindia.in

2

Rural Women Empowerment and Entrepreneurship Development

Prof. P. Mohan Reddy*
G. Venkatachalam**

ABSTRACT

The emergence of women entrepreneurs and their contribution to the national economy is quite visible in India. The number of women entrepreneurs has grown over a period of time, especially in the 1990s. Women entrepreneurs need to be lauded for their increased utilisation of modern technology, increased investments, finding a niche in the export market, creating a sizable employment for others and setting the trend for other women entrepreneurs in the organized sector. While women entrepreneurs have demonstrated their potential, the fact remains that they are capable of contributing much more than what they already are. Women's entrepreneurship needs to be studied separately for two main reasons. The first reason is that women's entrepreneurship has been recognised during the last decade as an important untapped source of economic growth. Women entrepreneurs

* Prof. P. Mohan Reddy, Department of Commerce, S.V., University, Tirupati, A.P.

** G. Venkatachalam, Research Scholar, Department of Commerce, S.V., University, Tirupati, A.P.

create new jobs for themselves and others and also by being different. They also provide the society with different solutions to management, organization and business problems as well as to the exploitation of entrepreneurial opportunities. The second reason is that the topic of women in entrepreneurship has been largely neglected both in society in general and in the social sciences. Not only have women lower participation rates in entrepreneurship than men but they also generally choose to start and manage firms in different industries than men tend to do. Economic empowerment, Improved standard of living, Self-confidence, Enhance awareness, Sense of achievement, Increased social interaction, Engaged in political activities, Increased participation level in gram sabha meeting, Improvement in leadership qualities, Involvement in solving problems related to women and community, Decision-making capacity in family and community.

INTRODUCTION

The emergence of women entrepreneurs and their contribution to the national economy is quite visible in India. The number of women entrepreneurs has grown over a period of time, especially in the 1990s. Women entrepreneurs need to be lauded for their increased utilisation of modern technology, increased investments, finding a niche in the export market, creating a sizable employment for others and setting the trend for other women entrepreneurs in the organized sector. While women entrepreneurs have demonstrated their potential, the fact remains that they are capable of contributing much more than what they already are. Women's needs to be studied separately for two main reasons. The first reason is that women's entrepreneurship has been recognised during the last decade as an important untapped source of economic growth. Women entrepreneurs create new jobs for themselves and others and also by being different. They also provide the society with different solutions to management, organization and business problems as well as to the exploitation of entrepreneurial opportunities. The second reason is that the topic of women in entrepreneurship has been largely neglected both in society in general and in the social sciences. Not only have women lower participation rates in entrepreneurship than men but they also generally choose to start and manage firms in different industries than men tend to do.

Development of the society is directly related with the Income Generation apacity of its members with agriculture, as the key income generation activity the entrepreneurship on farm and home can directly affect the income of a major chunk of our population. The growth of modernization processes such as industrialization, technical change; urbanization and migration further encourage it. Entrepreneurship on small-scale is the only solution to the problems of unemployment and proper utilisation of both human and non-human resources and improving the living condition of the poor masses [Prabha Sigh, 2009]. [Kuratka and Richard 2001] in their book on entrepreneurship started that entrepreneurship is the dynamic process of creating incremental wealth. This wealth is created by individuals who take the major risks in terms of equity, time and career commitment of providing value to some products or services the product or service itself may or my not be new or unique but value must some how be infused by the entrepreneur by securing and allocating the necessary skill and resources. The delivery of micro finance to the poor is smooth; effective and less costly if they are organized into Self-help Groups.

Self-help Groups is promoting micro-enterprise through micro-credit intervention. Micro-enterprise is an effective instrument of social and economic development. The micro-finance is agenda for empowering poor women. Micro-enterprises are an integral part of planned strategy for securing balanced development of the economy of the poor women. Rural women's participation in agro-based activities is much more than what statistics reveal. This is mainly due to the fact that most of the work done by the women at farm and home is disguised as daily chores. Mechanization and easy availability of labour provide more time to energetic women to engage themselves in self-employment or entrepreneur ventures. Rural women are having human and nonhuman resources to take up an enterprise need one an innovative mind and motivation. Entrepreneurship is the only solution to the growing employment among rural youth. It helps to generate employment for a number of people within their own social system. This is more beneficial for women in rural areas as it enables them to add to the family income while taking care of their own home and livestock centered task. Rural women possess abundant resources to take up enterprises. She has the benefit of easy availability of arm and livestock based raw materials and other resources.

Hence, she can effectively undertake both the production and processing oriented enterprises. Entrepreneurship development among rural women helps to enhance their personal capabilities and increase decision-making status in the family and society as a whole.

ENTREPRENEURSHIP DEVELOPMENT OF RURAL WOMEN THROUGH SELF-HELP GROUPS

Women comprise half of human resources they have been identified as key gents of sustainable development and women's equality is as central to a more hoslistic approach towards stabilizing new patterns and process of development that are sustainable. [Birendra Kumar Jha, 2009]. The contribution of women and their role in the family as well as in the economic development and social transformation are pivotal. Women constitute 90 per cent of total marginal workers of the country. Rural women who are engaged in agriculture form 78 per cent of all women in regular work [Harendar Kumar, 2009]. Experience of NIRD action research projects reveal that, the operational aspects, such as the extent of enabling that goes into the community self-help processes and sharpening the mind set of women. Men and the project administrators are low or critical components that determine their extent to which empowerment may or may not take place. The role of micro-credit is to, improve the socio and economic development of women and improve the status of women in households and communities. The micro-entrepreneurships are strengthening the women empowerment and remove the gender inequalities. Self-help Group's micro-credit mechanism makes the members to involve in other community development activities. Micro-credit is promoting the small-scale business enterprises and its major aim is to alleviate poverty by income generating activities among women and poor.

Therefore, they could achieve self-sufficiency. Now-a-days economic development is one of the factors that have changed the entire scenario of social and cultural environment within the country especially for the women. The rural women are engaged in small-scale entrepreneurship programme with the help of Self-help Groups. Through that they were economically empowered and attaining status in family and community. Rural women play a vital role in farm and home system. She contributes substantially in the physical aspect of farming, livestock management, post harvest and allied activities. Her direct and indirect contribution at the farm and home level along with livestock management operation has not only help to save their assets but also led to increase the family income. She performs various farm, livestock, post harvest and allied activities and possesses skills and indigenous knowledge in these areas. The women were empowering themselves technically to cope with the changing times and productively using their free time and existing skills for setting and sustaining enterprises. They were engaged in starting individual or collective income generation programme with the help of self-help group. This will not only generate income for them but also improve the decision-making capabilities that led to overall empowerment.

AREAS OF MICRO-ENTERPRISE DEVELOPMENT

Depending on number of factors ranging from land-holdings, subsidiary occupations, agro climatic conditions and socio-personal characteristics of the rural women and her family member the areas of micro-enterprises also differ from place to place. The micro enterprises are classified under three major heads:

1. Micro Enterprise Development Related to Agriculture and Allied Agricultural Activities

Like cultivating to organic vegetables, flowers, oil seeds and seed production are some of the areas besides taking up mushroom growing and bee – keeping. Some more areas can be like dehydration of fruits and vegetables, canning or bottling of pickles, chutneys, jams, squashes, dairy and other products that are ready to eat.

2. Micro-enterprise Development Related to Livestock Management Activities

Like diary farming, poultry farm, livestock feed production and production of vermi composting using the animal waste can be an important area in which women can utilise both her technical skills and raw materials from the farm and livestock to earn substantial income and small scale agro-processing units.

3. Micro-enterprise Development Related to Household Based Operations

Like knitting, stitching, weaving, embroidery, bakery and flour milling, petty shops, food preparation and preservation.

ADVANTAGES OF ENTREPRENEURSHIP AMONG RURAL WOMEN

Empowering women particularly rural women is a challenge. Micro-enterprises in rural area can help to meet these challenges. Micro-enterprises not only enhance national productivity, generate employment but also help to develop economic independence, personal and social capabilities among rural women. Following are some of the personal and social capabilities, which were developed as result of taking up enterprise among rural women.

Economic empowerment, Improved standard of living, Self-confidence, Enhance awareness, Sense of achievement, Increased social interaction, Engaged in political activities, Increased participation level in gram sabha meeting, Improvement in leadership qualities, Involvement in solving problems related to women and community, decision-making capacity in family and community.

CONCLUSION

Women's entrepreneurship is both about women's position in society and about the role of entrepreneurship in the same society. Women entrepreneurs faced many obstacles specifically in market their product (including family responsibilities) that have to be overcome in order to give them access to the same opportunities as men. In addition, in some countries, women may experience obstacles with respect to holding property and entering contracts. Increased participation of women in the labour force is a prerequisite for improving the position of women in society and self-employed women. Particularly the entry of rural women in micro enterprises will be encouraged and aggravated. Rural women can do wonders by their effectual and competent involvement in entrepreneurial activities. The rural women are having basic indigenous knowledge, skill, potential and resources to establish and manage enterprise. Now, what is the need is knowledge regarding accessibility to loans, various funding agencies procedure regarding certification, awareness on government welfare programmes, motivation, technical skill and support from family, government and other organization. More over Formation and strengthening of rural women Entrepreneurs network must be encouraged. Women entrepreneur networks are major sources of knowledge about women's entrepreneurship and they are increasingly recognised as a valuable tool for its development and promotion. This network helps to give lectures, printed material imparting first hand technical knowledge in production, processing, procurement, management and marketing among the other women. This will motivate other rural women to engage in micro entrepreneurship with the right assistance and they can strengthen their capacities besides adding to the family income and national productivity.

REFERENCES

Ram Naresh Thakur (2009), "Rural Women Empowerment in India" in *Empowerment of Rural Women in India* Kanishka Publishers, New Delhi.

Shobana Nelasco and Junofy Antorozarina (2009), "Rural Women Empowerment through Self-help Groups" in *Empowerment of Rural Women in India* Kanishka Publishers, New Delhi.

Lipi (2009), "Women Empowerment: Globalization and Opportunities" in *Empowerment of Rural Women in India* Kanishka Publishers, New Delhi.

Google.com

3

Empowerment of Women though Self-help Groups

Dr. Padmasree Karamala*
Dr. Bharathi Devi Anchula**

ABSTRACT

There are about 10 lakhs Women Self-help Groups (self-help groups) in Andhra Pradesh (AP) covering nearly 1 Crore of Poor Women. A.P., alone has about 60 per cent of self-help groups organized in the country. This self-help group movement is going rapidly in the state but some academic studies have found mixed results. In order to identify the real position, our paper assesses the working of self-help groups for women empowerment at five aspects that are: (i) Economic, (ii) Political, (iii) Psychological, (iv) Environmental, (v) Health and Social conditions.

INTRODUCTION

Empowering women is one of the important means of development. Nearly 80 per cent of the Indian Women lives in rural areas. Any assessment of the Economic empowerment of Indian Women can't afford to ignore studying the nature and extent of the Economic empowerment of rural women. Government introduced several women specific schemes for

* Head Department of Commerce, Y. V., University, Cadapah.

** Assistant Professor, Department of Economics ANU Campus, Ongole.

empowering women in general and rural women in particularly. Government programmes for women's development began early in 1954. One important scheme implemented since 1982 for the Economic uplift of women is the development of women and children of rural areas. Group strategy, training, awareness, generating promotion of marketing and income avenues has been given importance in the implementation of the programme. Government reports often mention that DWCRA scheme is working wonders in the context of empowering women Economically. Now this programmes terms as self-help groups.

SELF-HELP GROUP MOVEMENT IN ANDHRA PRADESH

The Government of Andhra Pradesh has take up the theme of women's empowerment as one of the strategies to tackle the socio-economic poverty. Self-help movement through savings has been take up as a mass movement by women a path chosen by them to shape this destiny for better.

The self-help groups, voluntarily formed by women save whatever amount they can save every month and mutually agree to contribute to a common fund to be lent to the members for meeting their productive and emergent credit needs. These groups are linked to the banks once their activities are stabilized. Besides focusing on entrepreneurial development of the beneficiaries, the self-help groups undertake the responsibility of delivering non-credit services such as literacy, health and environmental issues.

Each Self-help Group consists of 10-20 members. The members of self-help groups meet once or twice a month. There is a president, a secretary and a treasurer in each self-help group. The term of office bearers is on rotation basis, normally one year. All the groups maintain the records such as membership register, minutes book, savings ledger and the loan ledger. They prepare action plans after a detailed discussion of their proposed activities. Every member of the group gets an opportunity to put forth her views. Opinion of the majority is considered while arriving at important decisions. Thus the self-help groups have achieved success in bringing women to the mainstream of decision-making.

District wise details of self-help groups along with members in Andhra Pradesh on base of available secondary source of information has been presented in the below Table 3.1

Table 3.1: District wise details of self-help groups in andhra pradesh – 2010

S. No.	District Wise Data	No. of Self-help Groups	No. of Self-help group Members	AVG No. of Members for Self-help Group	Rounded Figures of Calum
1.	Adilabad	31.994	367.616	11.49	12
2.	Anantapur	48.435	473.773	9.78	10
3.	Chittoor	57.358	589.174	10.27	10
4.	East Godavari	79.312	767.614	9.68	10
5.	Guntur	48.141	455.419	9.56	10
6.	Hyderabad	98	991	10.11	10
7.	Cadapah	33.633	322.573	9.59	10
8.	Kammam	46.889	446.988	9.53	10
9.	Karimnagar	50.679	574.293	11.33	11
10.	Krishna	54.204	523.773	9.66	10
11.	Kurnool	38.632	405.110	10.49	11
12.	Mahaboobnagar	42.093	499.933	11.88	12
13.	Medak	37.286	418.628	11.23	11
14.	Nalgonda	50.006	526.238	10.52	11
15.	Nellore	34.334	330.829	9.63	10
16.	Nizamabad	34.998	369.946	10.57	11
17.	Prakasam	41.563	401.712	9.66	10
18.	Ranga Reddy	28.571	304.011	10.64	11
19.	Srikakulam	38.656	435.400	11.26	11
20.	Vishakapatnam	47.151	499.912	10.60	11
21.	Vijayanagaram	314.13	361.907	11.52	12
22.	Warangal	47.692	538.507	11.29	11
23.	West Godavari	57.169	548.732	9.60	10
	Total	**9,80,307**	**1,01,63,085**	**10.37**	**10**

Source: www.serp.com

From the above Table 3.1 it is noted that total number of self-help groups in the state as 9,80,307 with 1,01,63,085 members in the year 2010. And it is also observed average size of member for each self-help group in each district. At state level having 10.37 members of each self-help group. At all India level southern region having 64 per cent of self-help groups and in that south region A.P., having 60 per cent of self-help group but some Academic Studies have found mixed results of self-help groups in A.P., in order to identify the real position on women it is proposed to assess the working of self-help groups.

OBJECTIVES

1. To examine the nature of activities of self-help group members, finding, training facilities, marketing and income levels.
2. To assess improvement in the status and quality of life of poor women.
3. To assess the impact of self-help groups on empowerment of women.

METHODOLOGY

This study depends on the secondary source of data from Government reports, NABARD reports, publications, PhD., thesis's, and www.serp.org.in, www.google.com.

IMPACT OF SELF-HELP GROUPS ON WOMEN EMPOWERMENT

We have been selected to estimate empowerment of through the self-help groups as six aspects that are: *(i)* Economic, *(ii)* Political, *(iii)* Psychological, *(iv)* Environmental, *(v)* Health and *(iv)* Social Empowerment.

Sixty per cent of the women take up Economic activities related to agriculture and allied activities. Land lease for growing agricultural crop is a common practice in A.P., vegetable and flower cultivation, food crops and pulses, oil, seeds cultivation are taken up on leased lands. Similarly rearing of calves, ram lamp, chicks, piggery and duckery, dairy, value additions to milk products are preferred by women agriculture labourers. Illiterate and unskilled women engage in small business activities.

Public private partnership method is adopted in promoting Economic Opportunities to self-help group members by appointing them as dealers for the sale of products manufactured by enterprises. Companies in return train self-help groups in Finance Management, enterprise development, packing, branding and pricing of products. This partnership is a win model.

Nearly 20 per cent of self-help group members are artisans and engaged in making handicrafts and handloom products. And their Handicrafts, herbal, medicines and cosmetics, hand woven and embroiderer curtains, toys, paintings etc., are thus finding national and international markets, in this point of view self-help groups are encouraged to get PCs and software for accessing information and developing their business. Their products are photographed, scanned and displayed on websites, impact of this achievement on women as fallows.

Various organizations evaluated self-help groups. NGO universities, National Banks for agricultural and Rural Development (NABARD and ORG – Marg., some of the salient features.

- 98 per cent of the members make savings regularly as the norms prescribed by the groups.
- All the groups met at least once in a month to discuss various social issues related to their day-to-day life.
- 98 per cent of eligible members adopted small family norms.
- 100 per cent children of self-help groups members are able to access immunization services.
- 30 per cent of the members have access to safe cooking fuels (LPG) under the government promoted scheme popularly known as 'deepam'.
- 80 per cent of the total self-help groups have accessed financial assistance from banks and repayment is 98 per cent.

- In panchayat raj institutions 90 per cent of women elected to the local bodies.
- Members are engaged in 450 varieties of income-generated activities.
- Additional family incomes to member range from 1,000 – 5,000 per annum depending on the income generating activities.

MAJOR FINDINGS

The self-help groups have made a lasting impact on the lives of the women particularly in the rural areas of A.P. Their quality of life has improved a lot.

1. They could develop their skills and abilities in various productive activities.
2. There is an increase in their income, savings and consumption expenditure.
3. Increased self-reliance and self-confidence have improved the ability of women to mobilize various public services for their benefit.
4. They have become bold and can speak freely in front of big crows.
5. They can carry out any type of official work without any fear.
6. The social horizons of the members have also widened. They have made many friends and feel that now they are more popular and socially active.
7. The illiterate and semiliterate women have got a sense of satisfaction and wish fulfillment. Now they have become productive and the important members of the family.
8. They got high self-esteem, which enhances their capacity to work.
9. With improvements in women's economic opportunities and their ability to take collective action, there has been a significant decline in gender-based problems such as domestic violence, dowry, polygamy etc.

Interestingly, some of them are motivating other women to form self-help groups so that they also can reap the benefits. Thus the paper assess that the self-help groups are the effective instruments of women empowerment. The self-help groups have also created better understanding between the members of the different religious groups as the members of self-help groups belong to different religious. This is a welcome change to have understanding and tolerance towards the members of other religious particularly in a country like India where there is a diversity of religious and castes.

REFERENCES

Department of Rural Development Reports, 2009.

D. Jaya Kothaipillai, (1995), Women Empowerment, Gyan Publishing House, New Delhi, 1995.

Agarwal C.M., (2001), Indian Women, India Publishers and Distributors, Delhi.

Green's NGO (2010), Self-help Group Women in Prakasam District Reports Ongole.

N. Suneetha (2006), "Economic Empowerment of Women through DWCRA Scheme", Ph.D. Thesis, Department of Political Science, HCU, 2006.

Rambabu. G (2008), "Enterprise Promotion and Self-help Groups (SGHs) in Andhra Pradesh" Ph.D. Thesis, Department of Commerce, TU, Nizamabad.

Sathiabama K. (2010), Rural Women Empowerment and Entrepreneurship Development" Assess Student Papers, 2010

www. serp.org. in

www. google. com

4

Self-help Groups
A Silent Economic Revolution

Dr. S. Mansoor Rahman*
Dr. H. Akther Banu**
Dr. K. Chinna Venkataswamy***

ABSTRACT

Andhra Pradesh Government determined on two main aspects to concentrate more, they are Women Empowerment and Water Management. The progress is in favour of the state. Andhra Pradesh has achieved a record growth rate of 10.37 per cent in 2009. This is 1.57 per cent higher than that of the previous year. According to data released by the Central Statistical Organization, Andhra Pradesh has crossed the national average growth rate of 8.73 per cent. For the first time in its history, Andhra Pradesh has achieved a double-digit growth. This is because of the strong performance of all the sectors in the state. The state's performance exceeded the national average in every sector. The Overall development of the state is due to changing atmosphere in rural areas. The Self-help Groups play a

* Reader in Economics, Osmania College, Kurnool, A.P., E-mail: drmansoors@gmail.com; academymanpower.org@gmail.com

** Asst. Prof. and H.O.D., Kottam Engineering College, Kurnool, A.P., E-mail: akthermansoor17@gmail.com

*** Faculty, Rayalaseema University, Kurnool, A.P., E-mail: drmansoors@gmail.com

major role in transforming the rural economy. Micro-finance fulfils credit needs and helps the rural poor women to improve their standard of living. Hence the self-help groups are a new innovation in the field of rural development. The target of Micro-finance Institutions is to finance the rural women and thereby helping to transform rural economy by improving economic status of each and every household in the rural areas.

The concept of Self-help Groups (SHG) is not new. In 1954 the International Conference of Social Work had its main theme "Promoting Social Welfare through Self-help and Co-operative Action". The Dutch social worker J.E. Gejongh, has introduced the concept. Self-help Groups as an instrument for delivery mechanism of micro-finance is the brainchild of Grameena Bank of Bangladesh, which was founded by Prof. Mohammed Yunus of Chittagong University in the year 1975. The main characteristic features of Self-help Groups are participatory planning, holistic approach, resource mobilization, self-management, self-help and mutual help. The formation of Self-help Groups in India created awareness among women both in social and economic aspects. Self-help Groups approach to development is based essentially on the social mobilization model that is being advocated by different multilateral agencies. The failure of top to down beaurocratic approaches to rural development has necessitated the emergence of people based participation oriented strategy of development.

1. Empowerment of Women Through Self-help Groups

In any society, the status of women is an indicator of the level of its development. Women constitute nearly half of the total population and as such comprise nearly 50 per cent of the total human resources. The work participation rate for female is 25.7 per cent against the 39.2 per cent of total work force in Indian economy. Of which the work participation rate for female in rural areas has increased from 27.2 per cent in 1991 to 31.0 per cent in 2001, an increase by 3.8 per cent. But in the case of urban areas WPR increased from 9.7 per cent in 1991 to 11.0 per cent in 2001, an increase by only 1.7 per cent. Their contribution as home makers, wage - earners and citizens is crucial for the social and economic development of a country.

According to the annual report of Ministry of Rural Development, 11.45 lakhs of Self-help Groups have been formed in India so far. Therefore a social mobilization movement to mobilize rural poor woman on a massive scale, organize them in to groups, facilitate their capacity building to a stage where they would be able to effectively participate in the programme meant for them. Based on this experience a similar kind of movement was started in Andhra Pradesh in all the districts with thrift as an entry point for mobilization of rural poor women.

2. Delivery of Financial Services

The base strategy for IKP-DRDAs for promoting Self-help Group – Bank Linkage Programme is to ensure:

- Timely repayment of bank dues by groups financed earlier.
- Full participation Semi-urban and rural branches of banks.
- Coverage of all eligible fresh and repeat groups.
- Increase in per group finance and per branch linkage.
- Increase share of Self-help Group finance in District Credit Plan.
- Create the habit of savings.
- Doorstep savings and credit facilities to the poor.
- Exploitation of the untapped business potential in rural areas.

The Self-help Group – Bank Linkages is a great success story in A.P. 25 Commercial Banks, 16 Regional Rural Banks and more than 4150 branches are participating in the programme. Bank lending has dramatically increased from Rs. 197.70 Crores in 2001-02 to Rs. 5882.79 Crores in 2007-08. A.P., leads the country in Self-help Group – Bank Linkage Programme with 50 per cent of all bank loans given to Self-help Groups in India .The year wise progress up to March 2008-09 is given Table 4.1. During the year 2009-10, SERP has facilitated Rs. 5105.59 crores of bank loans to 3,29,545 Self-help Groups up to February 2010 as against the target of Rs. 9,000 crores.

Table 4.1: Self-help group-bank linkage programme

(Amount in Rs. Crore)

Year	Coverage of Groups	Amount of Assistance	Financing Branches	Per Group Finance	Per Branch Linkage
2000-01	84,939	143.12	3,058	16,580	28
2001-02	88,575	197.71	3,263	22,322	36
2002-03	1,65,429	454.12	3,701	27,506	45
2003-04	2,31,336	752.97	3,853	32,549	60
2004-05	2,94,179	1243.25	3.879	42,262	68
2005-06	2,88,711	2001.40	3,863	69,322	76
2006-07	3,66.489	3063.87	3,950	83,601	93
2007-08	4,31.515	5882.79	4,000	1,36,329	108
2008-09	4,37,003	7203.53	4,150	1,64,829	118

Source: SERP, 2009.

3. Interest Subsidy Programme – A Boon to Self-help Groups

The Government of Andhra Pradesh introduced Pavalavaddi Scheme (Interest Subsidy *i.e.* 0.25 per 100) during the year 2004-05 with an objective to provide interest subsidy on the Bank loans taken by the Self-help Groups in Andhra Pradesh to reduce the financial burden on them. The Scheme is applicable to all loans extended by banks on or after 01.07.2004, under Self-help Group – Bank Linkage Programme.

Self-help movement of women with thrift as entry point has grown as a mass movement in Andhra Pradesh. There are about 6.99 lakh women Self-help Groups covering nearly 89 lakh rural poor women in A.P., The Government adopted micro-credit as a tool to attain the economic empowerment of women and facilitated Self-help Group – Bank linkage programme in a big way since 1998-99 onwards in the State. The self-help group women have taken up various income generating activities by availing themselves of the facility under the Self-help Group – Bank Linkage programme and created a path for their economic empowerment. The Nationalized banks, Regional Rural Banks and Co-operative Banks are coming forward to issue loan to Self-help Groups.

The Banks are giving loans under Self-help Group Bank Linkage Programme with different rates of interest ranging from 8 per cent to 12 per cent. The groups are facing difficulty in paying such rates of interest. They reduce the financial burden on the Self-help Groups. The Government of Andhra Pradesh introduced the 'Pavala Vaddi' scheme (Interest Subsidy 0.25 per 100) during the year 2004-05 with an objective to provide interest subsidy on the loans taken by Self-help Groups under this scheme.

To encourage the women's groups further and also to achieve 100 per cent repayment, the State Government have introduced the 'Pavala Vaddi' scheme, where in the government is reimbursing the self-help group members any interest paid by the Self-help Groups over and above 3 per cent per annum. This has led to significant improvement in loan repayment. Under this initiative, 4,75,164 self-help groups were given Rs. 52.67 Crores in 2004-05 and 2005-06. 2,90,825 self-help groups were given Rs. 50.02 Crores during 2006-07 and 5,54,359 self-help groups were given Rs. 112.30 Crores during 2007-08 upto March 2008. During the year 2008-09, Rs. 195.31 crores interest subsidy was given to 7,14,930 groups. In the current financial year up to February 2010, an amount of Rs. 154.25 crores is given to 5.56 lakh groups. Thus, an amount of Rs. 564.25 Crores is given to 25.97 lakh self-help groups (repeat finance) as 'Pavala Vaddi' incentive from inception of the Scheme. The Self-help Group – Bank Linkages is a great success story in A.P. 25 Commercial Banks, 16 Regional Rural Banks and more than 4150 branches are participating in the programme.

Bank lending has dramatically increased from Rs. 197.70 Crores in 2001-02 to Rs. 5882.79 Crores in 2007-08. AP leads the country in Self-help Group – Bank Linkage Programme with 50 per cent of all bank loans given to self-help groups in India.

WOMEN EMPOWERMENT AND MICRO-FINANCE

The credit needs of the poor are essentially micro-credit needs. Micro-credit for the poor has gained importance as it could be used effectively to enhance their income and employment generating capacity. In this context, the self-help group is emerged to expand and it is a simplification of delivery mechanism of micro-credit for the poor. Many of them have achieved considerable success in providing micro-credit facilities to the members through bank linkage. By the turn of the century, the number of small borrowers from rural and semi-urban areas has crossed 200 million. Many state governments have recognised the importance of self-help groups and their role in delivering micro-credit. The NABARD and other commercial banks have also recognised self-help groups as their members. Self-help group as an instrument for delivery of micro-credit has multilateral benefits. Various studies have shown that Self-help Groups are formed by the women who have proved successful.

(i) Features of Micro-finance Institutions in India

The following are the important features of micro-finance institutions in India.

- About 60 per cent of MFIs are registered as societies.
- About 20 per cent are Trusts.
- About 65 per cent of the MFIs follow the operating model of self-help groups.
- 600 MFI initiatives have a cumulative outreach of 1.25 lakh crores poor households.
- NABARDs bank linkage programme has cumulatively reached a total of 9.4 lakh Self-help Groups with about 1.4 crores households.

(ii) Micro-finance institutions in Andhra Pradesh

Andhra Pradesh Mutually Aided Co-operative Societies (APMACS) Act 1995 has becoming a popular choice for formation MFI's in AP where they are based on cooperative principle, self-reliant, and have an aim of fulfilling the needs of its members. The act stipulates that cooperative may make its own by laws to guide its business and functioning. The only thing it has to ensure is that it works on the principles of cooperative and adheres to its rules and by laws.

Major demanders of the fund for serving the need of credit seekers:

- Share Micro-finance Limited (SML) (started in 1992 and incorporated as public limited company in April, 1999 in the form of an NBFC).
- Swayam Krishi Sangham (SKS) (incorporated in 1997).
- Pragati Seva Samithi (PSS).
- Star Youth Association (SYA).
- Spandana (Society and NBFC).
- Seva Micro-finance.
- Navajoythi.

Summing Up

Initially this programme was not successful because the government officials resisted and felt that it was not their job. This performance facilitated to understand the concept of Programme by the women. Taking advantage of this a team consisting of Mandal and Village officials accompanied the Kalajatha artists to motivate the self-help group formations. Basing on this approach the number of groups kept on increasing their members. The groups selected two members as leaders, had a group name of their own, opened a saving bank account in the nearest bank and members started saving *Rupee One* per day. The savings at the end of the month were deposited in the bank. It is interesting to note the reasons quoted by the groups for forming themselves as self-help groups. Groups saving led to a reinforcement of mutual trust that served the twin purpose of credit without conventional collateral and an inbuilt mechanism to ensure timely repayments through peer monitoring.

Dr. C.Rangarajan, the former Governor of the Reserve Bank of India has rightly pointed out that initiating and monitoring the credit programmes for the poor can be made more effective and less costly it banks make attempts to organize the poor in prompt repayment of loans. The self help groups can also contribute towards improving the quality of lending by offering loans in a prompt and simple manner, ensuring need-based loans and keeping the loan size within the repaying capacity of the borrowers. Undoubtedly, self help groups have the advantage of better knowledge about their members as compared to the bank staff.

The self-help groups play a major role in transforming the rural economy. Micro-finance fulfils credit needs and helps the rural poor to improve their standard of living. Hence the self help groups are a new innovation in the field of rural development to finance the rural women and thereby helping to transform rural economy by improving economic status of each and every household in the rural areas.

Finally, Women's earning have a positive correlation with children's health, nutrition levels and education. Studies have shown that Indian women contribute a much large share of their earning to basic family maintenance than men. The same success also proved in the case of Women Reservations in Local bodies. Women get 33 per cent reservation in *gram panchayat* and municipal elections. They raised their status with dignified dealings and administration, Now the Women's reservation bill was passed by the *Rajya Sabha* on 9 March 2010 by a majority vote of 186 members in favour and 1 against. It will now go to the *Lok Sabha*, and if passed there, would be implemented.

A Big Push can be seen in the upliftment of women of all fields. Certainly more women participation in politics and society is possible. Social norms in India strongly favour men, therefore, reservation for women is expected to create equal opportunity for men and women. Due to female foeticide and issues related to women's health, sex ratio in India is alarming at 1.06 males per female. It is expected this will change the society to give equal status to women.

At the same time women are supposedly more resistant to corruption. Therefore, this bill might prove to be a factor restraining the growth of corruption. The target of Micro-finance Institutions is to finance the rural women and thereby helping to transform rural economy by improving economic status of each and every household in the rural areas.

REFERENCES

Raka Gupta and Bipin-Kumar Gupta), Role of Women in Economic Deveopment, *Yojana,* August, 31, 1987.

Jayanthi, C, Women Entrepreneurs in the New Wave Economic Deveopment Programme. *Yojana,* August, 2003.

Misra, S.K, Puri, V.K, Indian Economy, Himalaya Publishing House, New Delhi, 2003.

Verma, S.B., Status of Women in Modern India, Deep and Deep Publications Pvt. Ltd., New Delhi, 2005.

Vijayeswari Rao, G, Women and Society, Himalaya Publishing House, Mumbai, 2004.

Deepak Walokar, Women Entrepreneurs, Himalaya Publishing House, Mumbai, 2001.

Muralidharan, K., The Globalized Women and Workforce: Issues, Problems and Solutions, University News, No. 43 (50), December, 12-18-2005.

Nirmala Banerjee and Poulomi Roy, What Does the State Do for Indian Women?, *Economic and Political Weekly,* October 30, 2004.

Mansoor Rahman, S. and Others, Women Entrepreneurship Development Through Self-help Group, Entrepreneurship Development Isues and Challenges (Ed), Allied Publishers, New Delhi 2007.

5

Problems of Women Entrepreneurs in India
An Overview

Dr. K. Jayachandra Reddy*
Dr. N. Praveen Kumar Reddy**
Mr. S. Dilli***

ABSTRACT

Women entrepreneurship development is an indispensable part of human resource development. The growth of women entrepreneurship is very low in India, particularly in the rural areas. Entrepreneurship amongst women has been a recent concern. Women have become aware of their existence their rights and their work situation. However, women of middle class are not too eager to alter their role in fear of social backlash. The progress is more visible among upper class families in urban cities. The present paper focuses on women entrepreneur's problems when they ventured out to shape their own position in the cutthroat world of business atmosphere.

The speed of the economic development of a nation primarily depends on the degree of developments in the

* Associate Professor, Department of Commerce, S.V.U.P.G., Centre, Kavali, Nellore, A.P.

** Professor of Management, Aurora's Scientific and Technological Institute (ASTI), Hyderabad, A.P.

*** Research Scholar, Department of Commerce, S.V.U.P.G., Centre, Kavali, Nellore, A.P.

Agricultural, Industrial and Service sectors. However, the developed as well as the developing countries today rely much upon the rapid industrialization on which their economic development depends. Accelerating industrial development through faster industrialization by exploitation and effective utilisation of the rich natural and physical resources, our country is endowed with, is a vital factor to faster economic development of our country. The role the people and their abilities have to play in this stupendous endeavour is supremely important, and that any negligence of the human factor would only enfeeble the economic prosperity of the country. Consequently, the industrial policies of the Government and the successive Five-year plans reiterate the Government's intention to stimulate and promote the human factor in industrial development. Thus, the entrepreneur has come to assume an important place and become the nerve centre of all economic activity.

The human beings have been enterprising since the dawn of history and this spirit, which was, transformed him as an entrepreneur to contribute for the economic prosperity of the country. The development of entrepreneurship, which is a human activity, has become imperative in the economic development and prosperity of our country. In this process man stands at the centre as organizer of human and exchange agent. Of these various roles he has to play, his function as an organizer of human and material resources is the most important and pivotal to ensure progress. Without his role the resources of production remain stationary and can never be transformed into products or services.

The spirit of enterprise makes man a spry entrepreneur. It is this spirit, which has transformed him over the centuries from a nomad into a cattle-rarer, an agriculturist, a trader, and an industrialist. Entrepreneurs are persons who intimate, organize, manage and control the affairs of a business unit, which combines the factors of production to supply goods and services. They are the nucleus of economic activity and propellers of economic development. In a developing economy such as India, entrepreneurs should be competent to perceive new opportunities, willing to take risks in exploring them and undergo, if necessary, rigorous hardships of the business. Entrepreneurship and economic development are closely bound with each other. Entrepreneurs are a dynamic force in the economic life of a society and are organizers of its productive resources. The development of right entrepreneurship is one of the most acute problems of the developing countries. In fact lack of the right kind of entrepreneurs in sufficient numbers is a factor hindering economic development of any country.

Entrepreneurship is vital input to industrial development, which has to depend invariably on entrepreneurial talent and efficiency. It has emerged as a major new force for economic change. The small-scale sector, which has gained momentum in the context of global economic change, needs qualitative and dynamic entrepreneurship as it contributes to the economic development of the country and nation building. The country, which has sound entrepreneurship, can progress in all spheres of the economy, as it can transform all available resources into valuable products. The progress of a developing country like India is bound up with enthusiastic and entrepreneurs who are committed to maximise the production as well as profitability of their organizations. Tapping the many untapped and locally available resources is the dire need of the day. And they have to be effectively utilised in manufacturing goods and services by applying an innovative scientific approach. Further to accelerate industrial production and augment the economic prospects of our country the young and energetic educated unemployed youth have to be motivated for the great task. In this endeavour along with men, women also have to be motivated and encouraged to contribute their mite to the economic progress of our country, as they have the potentiality to work hard with commitment and devotion.

Entrepreneurship requires the ability to take risk and coordinate the factors of production towards prosperity in an uncertain environment. As a matter of fact, entrepreneurs and their entrepreneurial qualities make all the difference in the success and failure of organizations. This fact has been widely realised by the planners. Therefore it is necessary to bring out the latent energies and talents of prospective entrepreneurs and mould them into active and responsible entrepreneurs who can transform the factors of production into economic products and services.

Women entrepreneurship development is an essential part of human resource development. The development of women entrepreneurship is very low in India, especially in the rural areas. Entrepreneurship amongst women has been a recent concern. Women have become aware of their existence their rights and their work situation. However, women of middle class are not too eager to alter their role in fear of social backlash. The progress is more visible among upper class families in urban cities.

The Government of India has undertaken a number of programmes where in entrepreneurs are trained on all, technical, managerial and other related skills so that they may enter the industrial field confidently with risk bearing capacity and manage their units on scientific lines. In this context it is important to recognise that in entrepreneurship development equal importance has to be given to potential and prospective women entrepreneurs. In view of the important role women can play in the industrial scene, the Government of India is encouraging them and trying to bring them into the fold of industrial activity. But it seems that women have not responded as favourably as expected. Probably, because custom and tradition are generally against their assuming new roles, which are mistakenly regarded as roles of men.

Women have a predominant role to play in the Indian economy and there is every need to bring them into the main stream of economic development, in general and industrial development in particular. They should be encouraged to free themselves from the shackles of conservative traditional customs, which confine them mostly to household activities. In view of their capacity for hard work, commitment, and sense of responsibility they should be properly motivated and their talents and abilities have to be nurtured. In the small-scale industrial sector there is considerable scope for their gainful employment and they can improve their standard of living, their own as well as that of people in general. But as the situation now prevails, there is no perceptible improvement in the development of women entrepreneurship. It is most unfortunate because, in India's population, women are on par with men. But their participation in economic activity and share of income in the total resources of the country, both are very low.

In spite of the measures taken by the Government for creating a congenial atmosphere to encourage women entrepreneur, the development of their entrepreneurship in our country is still far behind expectations. The overall industrial situation in our country is discouraging particularly in the small-scale sector where a majority of the units are in a moribund state, because of a conspicuous lack of managerial and innovative skills. Above all, the entrepreneurs are afraid that all small units will land in troubles due to industrial sickness, which is a quite serious problem in India. This situation naturally discourages prospective entrepreneurs, particularly women. Therefore, it is absolutely necessary that the entrepreneurs are properly motivated, encouraged, trained in technical and managerial skills, and provided with adequate financial resources for their successful functioning.

It may be taken as axiomatic that there can be no industrial development at all without a commensurate development of entrepreneurship in the small-scale sector particularly among women. While the Government has become aware of the need to develop women entrepreneurship and has taken several steps to promote it, the desired results have yet to be achieved. Part of the blame should lie with the prospective entrepreneurs themselves and part with the milieu in which they find themselves. If lack of will power, self-confidence, proper motivation, foresight, lack of awareness of opportunities, managerial skills, technical and financial support, and want of family and community support etc., stand in the way of a women entrepreneur, cumbersome formalities in starting an industry, lack of required infrastructural facilities, and assured marketing for their products, absence of proper training and encouragement from the Government, financial and other related agencies etc., discourage one from entrepreneurship. This situation has to be remedied if there should be rapid industrial development. The major problems faced by the women entrepreneurs in India are highlighted hereunder.

Indian Women Entrepreneurs Problems

Women Entrepreneurs in India are faced many problems to get ahead in their business life. Such as:

- The supreme restriction to women entrepreneurs is that they are women. Male members think it a big risk financing the ventures run by women.
- The financial institutions are skeptical about the entrepreneurial abilities of women. The bankers consider women loonies as higher risk than men loonies. The bankers put unrealistic and unreasonable securities to get loan to women entrepreneurs.
- The women entrepreneurs are suffering from inadequate financial resources and working capital. The women entrepreneurs lack access to external funds due to their inability to provide tangible security. Very few women have the tangible property in hand.
- Women's family obligations also bar them from becoming successful entrepreneurs in both developed and developing nations. "Having primary responsibility for children, home and older dependent family members, only few women can devote all their time and energies to their business".
- Indian women give more emphasis to family ties and relationships. Married women have to make a fine balance between business and home. More over the business success is depends on the support the family members extended to women in the business process

and management. The interest of the family members is a determinant factor in the realization of women folk business aspirations.

- Another argument is that women entrepreneurs have low-level management skills. They have to depend on office staffs and intermediaries, to get things done, especially, the marketing and sales side of business.
- The male – female competition is another factor, which develop hurdles to women entrepreneurs in the business management process.
- Knowledge of alternative source of raw materials availability and high negotiation skills are the basic requirement to run a business. Getting the raw materials from different sources with discount prices is the factor that determines the profit margin. Lack of knowledge of availability of the raw materials and low-level negotiation and bargaining skills are the factors, which affect women entrepreneur's business adventures.
- Knowledge of latest technological changes, know how, and education level of the person are significant factor that affect business. Because the literacy rate of women in India is found at low level compared to male population.
- Low-level risk taking attitude is another factor affecting women folk decision to get into business. Low-level education provides low-level self-confidence and self-reliance to the women folk to engage in business, which is continuous risk taking and strategic cession making profession. Investing money, maintaining the operations and ploughing back money for surplus generation requires high risk taking attitude, courage and confidence.
- Achievement motivation of the women folk found less compared to male members.
- Finally high production cost of some business operations adversely affects the development of women entrepreneurs.

Suggestions to Develop Women Entrepreneurs

Right efforts on from all areas are required in the development of women entrepreneurs and their greater participation in the entrepreneurial activities. Following efforts can be taken into account for effective development of women entrepreneurs.

- Believe women as specific target group for all developmental programmers.
- Improved educational facilities and schemes should be extended to women folk from government part.
- Sufficient training programme on management skills to be provided to women community and encourage women's participation in decision-making.
- Professional training to be provided to women community that enables them to understand the production process and production management.
- Programmes of training and counseling through the aid of committed NGOs, psychologists, managerial experts and technical personnel to be organized on a large scale of existing women entrepreneurs to remove psychological causes like lack of self-confidence and fear of success and they should be monitored continuously.
- Area of operations in which women are trained should focus on their marketability and profitability. And also making provision of marketing and sales assistance from government part.
- State finance corporations and financing institutions should permit by statute to extend purely trade related finance to women entrepreneurs.
- The financial intermediaries should provide more working capital assistance both for small scale venture and large scale ventures through micro credit system and enterprise credit system to the women entrepreneurs at local level.
- Infrastructure, in the form of industrial plots and sheds, to set up industries is to be provided by state run agencies.

- District Industries Centres and Single Window Agencies should active and liberal role in assisting women in their trade and business guidance and the programmes for encouraging entrepreneurship among women are to be extended in their jurisdiction.
- At the high school level the training in entrepreneurial attitudes should start through well-designed courses, which build confidence through behavioural games.
- More governmental schemes to be introduced to motivate women entrepreneurs to engage in small scale and large-scale business ventures through financial, technical, managerial, infrastructural assistances etc.

Conclusion

Entrepreneurship among women, no doubt improves the wealth of the nation in general and of the family in particular. Women today are more willing to take up activities that were once considered the preserve of men, and have proved that they are second to no one with respect to contribution to the growth of the economy. Women entrepreneurship must be moulded properly with entrepreneurial traits and skills to meet the changes in trends, challenges global markets and also be competent enough to sustain and strive for excellence in the entrepreneurial arena.

REFERENCES

Andrea Sith –Hunter., 2003. Diversity and Entrepreneurship: Analysing Successful Women Entrepreneurs. Paperback: Rowman and Little Field.

AWCF., (1999), A Development Link: A Look At Women Cooperatives and The Community. Manila, Asian Women in Cooperative Development Forum.

Bang Jee Chun, Women Entrepreneurs in SMEs in the APEC Region, APEC,. Jeanne Downing., 1992. The Growth and Dynamics of Women Entrepreneurs in South Africa (Gemini Technical Report). NTIS.

Medha Dubhashi Vinze., (1987), Women Entrepreneurs in India (A Socio-economic Study of Delhi 1975-85). South Asia Books.

Dhameja S K (2002), Women Entrepreneurs: Opportunities, Performance, Problems, Deep Publications Pvt. Ltd., New Delhi, p. 11.

Rajendran N. (2003), "Problems and Prospects of Women Entrepreneurs" SEDME, Vol. 30 No. 4 Dec.

Rao Padala Shanmukha (2007), "Enterpreneurship Development among Women: A Case Study of Self-help Groups in Srikakulam District, Andhra Pradesh" *The Icfai Journal of Enterpreneurship Development,* Vol. 1V, No. 1.

Sharma Sheetal (2006), "Educated Women, Powered, Women" *Yojana* Vol. 50, No. 12.

Website

www. googlee.co. in

www. wikipedia.com

6

Women Empowering through Self-help Groups
Role of Distance Education

Prof. P. Mohan Reddy*
Dr. L. Rajani**
Dr. Y. Subbarayudu***

ABSTRACT

Self-help Group (SHG) is a small voluntary association of poor people, preferably from the same socioeconomic background. They come together for the purpose of solving their common problems through self-help and mutual help. The self-help group promotes small savings among its members. The growing social awareness across the globe has brought a number of issues to the fore among which gender equality and empowerment of women are very significant. Discrimination against women in the form of male-female differentiation constitutes the core of the gender-biased system. The education is the biggest liberating force and the rise in the levels of education which nourishes progressive outlook and the advent of industrialization and modernization have effected a sea change in the attitudes and thinking pattern of the people. The empowerment is not

* Professor, Department of Commerce, S.V., University, Tirupati, A.P.

** Academic Consultant, Department of Commerce, Yogi Vemana University, Kadapa, A.P.

*** Assistant Professor, Department of HRM, Yogi Vemana University, Kadapa, A.P.

essentially political alone in fact; political empowerment will not succeed in the absence of economic empowerment. The scheme of micro-financing through Self-help Groups (SHG) has transferred the real economic power in the hands of women and has considerably reduced their dependence on men. This has helped in empowerment of women and building self-confidence, but lake of education often comes in the way and many a times they had to seek help from their husbands for day-to-day work viz; bank, accounts, etc. Alternative perspectives in education and training constitute a major item in the agenda set out for the distance education system. The distance education provides an opportunity to these women to improve their skills. The higher level of learning will help them to learn skill and vocations and play an effective role in the management of self-help groups. I suggest the differential rate of interest for women doing any course through Open Schools. The economic incentives and effective NGOs participation will definitely make the women empowerment a reality from a distant dream at present.

INTRODUCTION

While no definitive date has been determined for the actual conception and propagation of self-help groups, the practice of small groups of rural and urban people banding together to form a savings and credit organization is well established in India. In the early stages, NGOs played a pivotal role in innovating the self-help group model and in implementing the model to develop the process fully. In the 1980s, policy makers took notice and worked with development organizations and bankers to discuss the possibility of promoting these savings and credit groups. Their efforts and the simplicity of self-help groups helped to spread the movement across the country. State governments established revolving loan funds which were used to fund self-help groups. By the 1990s, self-help groups were viewed by state governments and NGOs to be more than just a financial intermediation but as a common interest group, working on other concerns as well. The agenda of self-help groups included social and political issues as well. The spread of self-help groups led also to the formation of self-help group Federations which are a more sophisticated form of organization that involve several self-help groups forming into Village Organizations (VO)/Cluster Federations and then ultimately into higher level federations (called as Mandal Samakhya (MS) in AP or self-help group Federation generally). Self-help Group Federations are formal institutions while the self-help groups are informal. Many of these self-help group federations are registered as societies, mutual benefit trusts and mutually aided cooperative societies. Self-help Group Federations resulted in several key benefits including:

- Stronger political and advocacy capabilities.
- Sharing of knowledge and experiences.
- Economies of scale.
- Access to greater capital.

Some states have developed self-help groups further than others. This report is based on the experience that APMAS has had in working with self-help groups in Andhra Pradesh and limited experiences in other states. Self-help Group (SHG) is a small voluntary association of poor people, preferably from the same socio-economic background. They come together for the purpose of solving their common problems through self-help and mutual help. The self-help group promotes small savings among its members. The savings are kept with a bank. This common fund is in the name of the self-help group. Usually, the number of members in one self-help group does not exceed twenty.

STRUCTURE OF SELF-HELP GROUP

A self-help group is a group of about 10 to 20 people, usually women, from a similar class and region, who come together to form savings and credit organization. They pooled financial resources to make small interest bearing loans to their members. This process creates an ethic that focuses on savings first. The setting of terms and conditions and accounting of the loan are done in the group by designated members.

AIM OF THE PAPER

Aim of the paper is divided into three parts. In the first parts we shall discuss the concept of Self-help Groups (SHGs) as an instrument of economic empowerment, its various models and the strength of informal sector over formal sector. In second part we shall present the progress of the Self-help Group – Bank led model of micro-financing in India, and finally we shall conclude with the presentation of strategy of women empowerment by linking benefits extended by the governments to the members of Self-help Groups (SHGs) with open and distance education, degrees or diplomas.

SELF-HELP GROUP – A CONCEPT

The origin of self-help groups is from the brainchild of Grameen Bank of Bangladesh, which was founded by Mohammed Yunus. Self-help Groups were started and formed in 1975. In India NABARD is initiated in 1986-87. A Self-help Group (SHG) has an average size of about 15 people from a homogeneous class. They come together for addressing their common problems. They are encouraged to make voluntary thrift on a regular basis. They use this pooled resource to make small interest bearing loans to their members. The process helps them imbibe the essentials of financial intermediation including prioritisation of needs, setting terms and conditions, and accounts keeping. This gradually builds financial discipline in all of them. They also learn to handle resources of a size that is much beyond individual capacities of any of them. The self-help group members begin to appreciate the fact that resources are limited and have a cost. Once the groups show this mature financial behaviour, banks are encouraged to make loans to the self-help group in certain multiples of the accumulated savings of the self-help group. The bank loans are given against group dynamics without any collateral and at market interest rates. The groups continue to decide the terms of loans to their own members. Since the groups' own accumulated savings are part and parcel of the aggregate loans made by the groups to their members, peer pressure ensures timely repayments. Apart from financial help at the time of need, the group provides social security to its members.

Micro-finance programmes are currently being promoted as a key strategy for simultaneously addressing both poverty alleviation and women's empowerment. Before 1990s, credit schemes for women were almost negligible. There were certain misconception about the poor people that they need loan at subsidized rates of interest on soft terms, they lack skills, capacity to save, credit worthiness and therefore are not bankable. Nevertheless, the experiences of several and self-help groups reveal that rural poor are actually efficient managers of credit and finance. Availability of timely and adequate credit is essential for them in their enterprises rather than subsidies. Earlier government efforts through various poverty alleviation schemes for self-employment by providing credit and subsidy received little success. Since most of them were target based involving various government agencies and banks.

MEANING OF EMPOWERMENT

Empowerment is not giving people power, people already have plenty of power, in the wealth of their knowledge and motivation, to do their jobs magnificently. It encourages people to gain the skills and knowledge that will allow them to overcome obstacles in life or work environment and ultimately, help them develop within themselves or in the society. The Scheme of Micro-financing through self-help groups create empowerment promoting conditions for women to move from positions of marginalisation within household decision-making process and exclusion within community, to one of greater centrality, inclusion of voice. The Social processes of Micro-financing programmes strengthens women's self-esteem and self-worth, instill a greater sense of awareness of social and political issues leading to increased mobility and reduced traditional seclusion of women.

Most importantly micro-finance programmes enable women to contribute to the household economy, increasing their intra-household bargaining power. Thus, micro financing through Self-help groups has transferred the real economic power in the hands of women and has considerably reduced their dependence on men. But the lack of education often comes in the way and many a times they had to seek help from their husbands or any other educated man/woman for day-to-day work. The political as well as economic empowerment will not succeed in the absence of women education in skills and vocations they require the most. The Governments in developing countries therefore must take effective steps to enroll the members of self-help groups in the schemes of open schooling or any other distance mode to impart education. Although it is also true that economic empowerment alone does not always lead to reversal in gender relationship.

DIFFERENT MODELS OF LINKAGE IN SELF-HELP GROUPS

Since the introduction of financial sector reforms in 1991 the banks are using these distinct linkage models to finance self-help groups.

- **Self-help Groups Formed and Financed by Banks**

In this model, banks themselves take up the work of forming and nurturing the groups, opening their savings accounts and providing them bank loans. Upto March 2006, 20 per cent of the total number of self-help groups financed were from this category. This showed an increase of 61.63 per cent in bank loan to self-help groups over the position as on March 05, reflecting an increased role of banks in promoting and nurturing self-help groups.

- **Self-help Groups Formed by Formal Agencies other than Banks, NGOs and Others, But Directly Financed by Banks**

This model continues to have the major share, with 74 per cent of the total number of self-help groups financed upto 31 March 2006 falling under this category. Here, NGOs and formal agencies in the field of micro-finance act only as facilitators. They facilitate organizing, forming and nurturing of groups, and train them in thrift and credit management. Banks give loans directly to these self-help groups.

- **Self-help Groups Financed by Banks Using NGOs and other Agencies as Financial Intermediaries**

This is the model wherein the NGOs take on the additional role of financial intermediation. In areas where the formal banking system faces constraints, the NGOs are encouraged to approach a suitable bank for bulk loan assistance. This, in turn, is used by the NGO for onlending to the self-help groups. In areas where a very large number of self-help groups have been financed by bank branches, intermediate agencies like Federations of self-help groups are coming up as links between bank branch and member self-help groups. These Federations are financed by banks, who, in turn, finance their member self-help groups. The share of cumulative number of self-help groups linked under this model upto March 06 continued to be relatively small at 6 per cent.

PROGRESS OF MICRO-CREDIT THROUGH SELF-HELP GROUPS IN INDIA

A pilot project for linking self-help groups with banks was launched by NABARD in 1992. The Reserve Bank of India persuaded Commercial Banks, Regional Rural Banks and Co-operative Banks to actively participate in the linkage programme. Under the RBI's guidelines, banks were given permission to open saving bank account in the name of self-help group, and relaxation of security requirements. Thus, an informal credit system was evolved with assistance from formal financial institutions. The agencies involved in the schemes were NABARD, Banks, NGOs and self-help groups members. The main objectives were to provide the following:

- Supplementary credit to self-help groups.
- Reductions in transactions cost for both banks as well as self-help groups by reducing paper work.
- To mobilize small savings among poor rural women.
- To build mutual trust and confidence between Banks, NGOs and rural poor.
- To create healthy relations between self-help groups members and linking agencies.
- Constant supervision and monitoring by banks through NGOs.

The Rashtriya Seva Samithi (RASS)

The RASS was established in 1981 at Tirupati. The activities and programmes of RASS were designed for the development of poor in the drought prone Rayalaseema districts of Andhra Pradesh. This region has a high percentage of population who belong to scheduled castes and the backward castes. The region does not have any major industries except a few agro-processing units It also lags behind other regions of the State aggravated poverty, unemployment and environmental degradation in the Rayalaseema region. Some of the anti-poverty programmes proved ineffective, as it was more on target achievement rather than human development. Moreover, the rural poor were not involved from the stage of planning to the stage of implementation and evaluation of programmes meant for their upliftment.

OBJECTIVES

The main objective of RASS was to adopt such a strategy, which would bring into fold the poor in the development process. The RASS, believes in the following:

- Involvement of poor in the entire process of development from planning to monitor.
- Identification of priorities by the poor themselves.
- Empowerment of women as a key to self-sustained development of the poor.
- Provision of community infrastructure as an essential precondition for self sustained growth.
- The RASS considers the following four interventions as crucial for the poor to reach the stage of social consciousness and empowerment.
- Human resource development (by way of massive education, skill up gradation, health services, safe drinking water, sanitation etc., for the disadvantaged groups).
- Self-management and momentum (for the promotion of saving and credit, community management of infrastructure, leadership and self-helped).

Area of Operation and Growth

The core area of operation of RASS includes the districts of Y.S.R, Anantpur, Kurnool and Chittoor. The initial activities of RASS were concentrated in Chittoor district, which accounts for an estimated population of 4.3 million. Subsequently, these activities were spread to other districts of Rayalaseema. Over a period of eighteen years, RASS has been successful in building up a large administrative infrastructure and reaching out to the rural poor in the backward areas within Andhra Pradesh and in the States of Orissa and Tamil Nadu. Because of its involvement in multi-faceted activities, several funding agencies at the national and international level have shown interest and confidence in RASS. Starting with three programme activities in eight villages with 15 staff members, RASS has acquired the status of a national level organization.

Women Centered Activities

To tap the potentialities and managerial capacities of rural women RASS has implemented several activities. RASS has been instrumental in organizing rural women to show their strength and defend themselves for their rights with the formation of Mahila Mandals. These Mandals work under the direct supervision and guidance of RASS and also, get regular information about Government programmes, bank financing, marketing trends etc. The successful working of Mahila Mandals has resulted in the formation of a large number of Self-help Groups (SHGs). For women to get gainful employment especially belonging to SC, ST and BCs, RASS provides training facilities and generates innovative programmes. The vocational skills, thus acquired, help women to be self-reliant.

Growth and Performance of Self-help Groups

The successful working of Mahila Mandals has resulted in the formation of a large number of Self-help Groups (SHGs). In 1990 with the help from RASS, 30 self-help groups were formed involving 10-15 women members. Within a year, there were 123 self-help groups with a total membership of 1559 women. A significant feature of this system was that a large number of women shifted their borrowing from traditional moneylenders to self-help groups at reasonable rates of interest. Moreover, RASS has lined with Rashtriya Mahila Kosh (RMK) and NABARD to mobilize funds. RASS has borrowed about Rs. 7 million from RMK and lent it to informal women groups. Along with the loan from RMK and their own savings, women groups have generated credit to the extent of Rs. 11 million.

STRATEGY OF WOMEN EMPOWERMENT

In view of low literacy rate of women and the gigantic task of educating rural women a suitable strategy will have to be planned. The major task is to identify the areas where these groups in fact, are facing problems because at this stage only the problem solving adult learning technique will attract these rural poor to improve their working and income. The success of any strategy of women empowerment depends upon the following factors:

1. Level of education, hard work.
2. Social custom.
3. Family planning, small family.
4. Health, medical services, cleanliness.
5. Environment, tree growing, kitchen gardening.

Various case studies show that there is a positive correlation between credit availability and empowerment of women.

On the face of it, Distance Education appears *per se* a 'women friendly' form of acquiring education and formal qualifications. There are two characteristics which are generally seen to render this mode of learning specially suitable for women, by making distance education compatible with other spheres of life, first, there is no attendance requirement, second, at the same time, there is a high degree of flexibility in learning schedules and time management. These characteristics have three distinct and undisputed advantages for the distant student. Since, the distance-teaching curriculum is designed for independent study if can well fit with family commitments and living at home. Learning material is sent to the women at their home or workplace they can learn while they earn and the NGO/ self-help group may provide them the required tuition wherever they desire. Rural women can learn at their own pace on the basis of availability of time. Technology helps them round the clock access on student support services. In rural India where girls and women are largely excluded from education at all levels D.E. may be the only option. Opportunities are not equal. Responsibilities are more they have to overcome greater odds, less support from their families, early marriage childcare. The members of self-help groups are mainly illiterate and do not have access to formal education. In a study it was reported that the members of the Groups were not fully literate and were not able to read and write. Many are now able to append their signatures perhaps an outcome of the government-sponsored literacy programme and the compulsion to affix signature on several occasions as members of self-help groups The handicap of literacy would be a hurdle for achieving many desired results. For example they will be unable to follow the accounts maintained by the group and hence remain ignorant about the amount pooled individually and in the group, and would be unable to draft an application to represent their case. It is therefore essential to provide them education through especially designed modules through distance education that are directly useful as a member of self-help group.

At this part they do not need school or university certificate, Diploma or degrees. They need improvement in their professional skills and solving their day-to-day problems in the working and functioning of self-help groups. They should be explained the advantage of group based strategies in poverty alleviation. Importance of savings and opening bank account, marketing of products, timely repayment and repeat loaning. It is important to explain that she is not alone and that such problems are being faced universally. Only by self-help they may fight against their misfortune and improve upon the fate of their family and children. All these problems, opportunities and chances can be explained the women through short duration training module delivered at their doorstep or work place. At the initial stage we may face certain problems and resistance from the participants if we demand some extra time and money. It is therefore suggested that the benefits should be linked with the DE modules and subsidies should be in the form of distance education and not cash. There are instances where cash subsidies were taken away forcefully by male, members in the family for liquor consumption and gambling and made no significant impact in the society. But education is such a type of subsidy that cannot be robbed by male members in the family. Secondly educated mother will further educate her children and thus will help in mitigating the curse of illiteracy and poverty from the society.

EDUCATION EMPOWERS WOMEN

Alternative perspectives in education and training constitute a major item in the agenda set out for the distance education system. It is also observed that open education at present is mainly catering to the needs of elites in the urban areas and it has to make in roads in rural areas where India lives. In rural areas women are totally dependent on men, as they do not have economic power to spend. The historical relationships with their husbands can be seen as influenced by historical factors that shape the social structures of how they are subordinated. It has been observed in several research studies that women do experience a double day, as they return to study combined with their domestic roles. The Policy planners must think to integrate the economic benefits with education. I suggest the Differential Rate of Interest (DIR) for women doing any Course through Open schools or any other mode of Open and Flexible learning.

Women Education is sometimes also perceived as a threat by their husbands. Studying is seen as changing the identity of the partner from being subservient and domesticated (Morgan 1995: 321). It has been noted that education as such serves to empower women. This may be on the most basic level through literacy programmes or on more advance levels through university study and even Ph.D., programmes. A UNICEF study (1998) on Violence against women in South East Asia concluded that compulsory schooling for all girls would be a long-term measure to reduce violence against women by providing them qualifications as the basis for getting a job which in turn will enable them to earn a their own income and improve their status. Thus the self-help groups should in-fact also be converted in to Self-help Study Groups that will give them not only enhanced income but also enhanced esteem and self-confidence to do something meaningful for the society as a whole. They should realize that they are not the isolated unproductive but important wheel for the smooth running of the society. The economic incentives and effective NGOs participation will definitely make the women.

CONCLUSION

Self-help Group (SHG) is a small voluntary association of poor people, preferably from the same socioeconomic background. They come together for the purpose of solving their common problems through self-help and mutual help. The self-help group promotes small savings among its members. The scheme of micro-financing through Self-help Groups (SHGs) has transferred the real economic power in the hands of women and has considerably reduced their dependence on men. This has helped in empowerment of women and building self-confidence, but lake of education often comes in the way and many a times they had to seek help from their husbands for day-to-day work *viz.*, bank, accounts, etc. The distance education provides an opportunity to these women to improve their skills. The higher level of learning will help them to learn skill and vocations and play an effective role in the management of self-help groups. Thus the self-help groups should in-fact also be converted in to Self-help Study Groups that will give them not only enhanced income but also enhanced esteem and self confidence to do something meaningful for the society as a whole. They should realize that they are not the isolated unproductive but important wheel for the smooth running of the society. The economic incentives and effective NGOs participation will definitely make the women. The Government must take effective measures to enroll the members of self-help groups in the schemes of Open Schooling. It is observed that open education at present is mainly catering to the needs of elites in the urban areas and it has to make inroads into rural areas where India lives. The Policy planners must think to integrate the economic benefits with education. I suggest the differential rate of interest for women doing any course through Open Schools. The economic incentives and effective NGOs participation will definitely make the women empowerment a reality from a distant dream at present.

REFERENCE

Morgan, A. (1995), 'Adult Change and Development: Learning and Peoples' Lives' in D. Sewart (ed.) One World.

Many Voices: Quality in Open and Distance Learning, Milton Keynes: ICDE, and the Open University.

Purohit, Sheela, "Micro-credit and Women Empowerment, http://www.gdre.org

Stewart, Aileen Mitchell. Empowering People (Institute of Management). London: Financial Times Management, 1994. Print.

Thomas, K. W. and Velthouse, B. A. (1990), Cognitive Elements of Empowerment: An 'Interpretive' Model of Intrinsic Task Motivation. *Academy of Management Review*, Vol. 15, No. 4, 666-681.

Dadhich, C.L. Lessons from the Micro-credit Experience of India, www.aproácha.th.com

Kamesan, Vepa (2003), " Indian Economic Scenario-Yesterday-Today-Tomorrow. Inaugural Address at Seminar on Banking – Agriculture Industry – IT-New Hopes – New Challenges Organized by Telugu Vaibhavam at Hyderabad, Sep. 16.

7

Women Entrepreneurship
Role of Self-help Groups

Dr. P.V. Narasaiah*
T. Sivasankar**
N. Venkatarathnam**
D. Banuchandra**

ABSTRACT

Women entrepreneurs are those women who think of a business enterprise, initiate it, organize and combine the factors of production, operate the enterprise and undertake risks and handle economic uncertainty involved in running a business enterprise. Women in India constitute around half of the country's population. Hence, they are regarded as the 'better half of the society'. In the official proclamation, they are at par with men. But, in real life, the truth prevails otherwise. Our society is still male-dominated and women are not treated as equal partners both inside and outside four walls of the house. In fact, they are treated as abala, i.e., weak and dependent on men. As such, the Indian women enjoy a disadvantageous status in the society. In the late 1990's evaluation reports of the Integrated Rural Development Programmes for creating self-employment opportunities in rural areas reflected the

* Professor, S.V., University, Tirupathi, A.P.

** Research Scholars, Department of Commerce, S.V., University, Tirupathi, A.P.

flaws in the implementation of the programme. This led the Central Government to announce a holistic programme called Swarna Jayanthi Gram Swarozgar Yogana (SGSY). This programme was based on a group (community) approach to rural development where the rural poor were organized in to Self-helf Groups (SHGs) and took up viable economic activities on their own on a sustainable basis with the support from government subsidy and bank credit. Women in India have been confronting many socio-economic problems which adversely affecting women entrepreneur skills and consequently making them weak. Hence all these problems need attention. Against this backdrop the paper attempts to evaluate the role of self-help groups in promoting women entrepreneurs in Kadapa district, a drought-prone area in A.P. In addition the paper also throws light on different problems of women entrepreneurs. The paper also strongly emphasizes the need for solving women entrepreneurial problems and making them omnipotent.

WOMEN ENTREPRENEURSHIP – AN OVERVIEW

Women constitute around half of the total world population. So is in India also. They are, therefore, regarded as the better half of the society. In traditional societies, they were confined to the four walls of houses performing household activities. In modern societies, they have come out of the four walls to participate in all sorts of activities. The global evidences buttress that women have been performing exceedingly well in different spheres of activities like academics, politics, administration, social work and so on. Now, they have started plunging into industry also and running their enterprises successfully.

CONCEPT OF WOMEN ENTREPRENEURS

Women entrepreneurs may be defined as a woman or group of women who initiate, organize and run a business enterprise. In terms of Schumpeterian concept of innovative entrepreneurs, women who innovate, imitate or adopt a business activity are called 'women entrepreneurs'. The Government of India has defined women entrepreneurs based on women participation in equity and employment of a business enterprise.

Accordingly, a women entrepreneur is defined as "an enterprise owned and controlled by a women having a minimum financial interest of 51 per cent of the capital and giving at least 51 per cent of the employment generated in the enterprise to women". However, this definition is subject to criticism mainly on the condition of employing more than 50 per cent women workers in the enterprises owned and run by the women.

In nutshell, women entrepreneurs are those women who think of a business enterprise, initiate it, organize and combine the factors of production, operate the enterprise and undertake risks and handle economic uncertainty involved in running a business enterprise.

Women in India constitute around half of the country's population. Hence, they are regarded as the 'better half of the society'. In the official proclamation, they are at par with men. But, in real life, the truth prevails otherwise. Our society is still male-dominated and women are not treated as equal partners both inside and outside four walls of the house. In fact, they are treated as abla, *i.e.*, weak and dependent on men. As such, the Indian women enjoy a disadvantageous status in the society. Let some facts be given. The much low literacy rate (40%), low work participation rate (28%) and low urban population share (10%) of women as compared to 60 per cent, 52 per cent and 18 per cent respectively of their male counterparts well confirm their disadvantageous position in the society. Our age old socio-cultural traditions and tools arresting the women within four walls of their houses also make their conditions more disadvantageous.

Women in India plunged into business for both occupation or venture with an urge to do something independently. Push factors refer to those factors which compel women to take up their own business to tide over their economic difficulties and responsibilities.

WOMEN ENTREPRENEURSHIP AND SELF-HELP GROUPS (SHGs)

In the late 1990's evaluation reports of the Integrated Rural Development Programmes for creating self-employment opportunities in rural areas reflected the flaws in the implementation of the programme. This led the Central Government to announce a holistic programme called Swarna Jayanthi Gram Swarozgar Yogana (SGSY). This programme was based on a group (community) approach to rural development where the rural poor were organized in to Self-Helf Groups (SHGs) and took up viable economic activities on their own on a sustainable basis with the support from government subsidy and bank credit. Self-help Groups were also formed under Swayam Siddha, Mission Shakti, Rashtriya Mahila Kosh (RMK), Self-help Group – Bank linkage scheme of National Bank for Agriculture and Rural Development (NABARD), Small Industries Development Bank of India (SIDBI) etc.

Self-help Groups are formed as small functional groups in rural areas to increase the resource base of the members through the act of thrift and credit among themselves. They raise their corpus with credit support from service area banks and subsidy from government agencies concerned. To create quality groups, rural participation plays a pivotal role in identifying its members who are brought into the self-help group-fold, though the process of social mobilisition functions of the groups are monitored and assessed by the external agencies with active support of Government, the lead bank of the region and panchayat union.

Self-help Group – Bank linkage programme has emerged as a cost effective strategy for banking with the poor. The programme has made big strides in the site and has helped many poor people come out of the clutches of money lenders and has helped the poor women folk to organize themselves besides bringing awareness among the rural women folk regarding various development programmes available for them. The experience of the bankers in financing self-help groups has been very encouraging and the programmes in reacting new heights in the site.

ABOUT THE PAPER

The present paper seeks to evaluate the role of self-help groups in promoting women éntrepreneurship in kadapa district, a drought-prone and backward area in the state of Andhra Pradesh.

METHODOLOGY

Both primary and secondary data have been collected to arrive at meaningful inferences. The secondary data for a five year period from 2005-06 to 2009-10 was collected from the authentic records of DRDA, Kadapa.

GROWTH OF SELF-HELP GROUPs IN KADAPA DISTRICT – A REVIEW

A modest attempt is made to review the growth of self-help groups in Kadapa district. Table 7.1 is given in this regard.

Table 7.1: Year-wise growth in self-help groups in kadapa district

Sl. No.	Year	No. of Groups	Growth % Increase (+) or Decrease (-)
1.	2005-06	22950	13.33
2.	2006-07	27693	20.66
3.	2007-08	31322	13.10
4.	2008-09	34890	11.39
5.	2009-10	35358	13.41

Source: Compiled from the records of DRDA, Kadapa.

It is evident from the Table 7.1 that there have been fluctuations in the growth of no. of self-help groups. However, during the year 2006-07 the growth rate had increased to around 21 per cent against 13 per cent in 2005-06. But drastically declined to 13.41 per cent by the end of the year

2009-10. It may be inferred that women are not coming forward to form themselves into self-help groups due to many socio-economic problems.

Table 7.2: Caste-wise break-up of self-help groups during the year 2009-10

Sl. No.	Category	No. of Groups	Average to Total
1.	Scheduled Tribes	914	4.10
2.	Scheduled Caste	7584	34.04
3.	Back ward classes	10828	48.60
4.	Minorities	2952	13.25
	Total	**22278**	**100.00**

Source: Ibid.

It is to note that the backward classes are large in number as for as self-help groups are concerned as shown by Table 7.2. This constitutes more than 40 per cent of the total. It is necessary to induce the scheduled tribes and minorities towards self-help groups.

Table 7.3: Financing of self-help groups by APGB and SBI

Sl. No.	Year	No. of Groups	Growth Rate (%)	Bank Loan (Rs. in Lakhs)	Growth Rate (%)
1.	2005-06	10491	–	6966.53	–
2.	2006-07	12742	21.45	10198.30	46.33
3.	2007-08	15526	21.84	20445.2	100.47
4.	2008-09	17855	15.00	21376.00	4.56

Source: Ibid.

It is apparent from the Table 7.3 the growth rates in terms of no. of groups and deployment of bank loans are not impressive. It is distressing to notice that the growth rates were sharply deteriorated during 2008-09.

ANALYSIS OF FIELD STUDY

Of the total self-help groups groups working in the district, 50 self-help groups have been selected at random for purpose of field study. The selection is made from the list of self-help groups provided by DRDA, Kadapa.

The division-wise break-up of self-help groups in Kadapa district are depicted in Table 7.4.

Table 7.4: Division-wise break-up of self-help groups

Division	No. of Self-help Groups	Percentage
Kadapa	13	26
Jammalamadugu	20	40
Rajampet	17	34
Total	**50**	**100**

Source: Field Study.

It is observed from the Table 7.4 the Jammalamadugu division ranks first, which accounts for 40 per cent of the total self-help groups formed in the district followed Rajampet division.

The details of caste wise break up of self-help groups of furnished in Table 7.5.

Table 7.5: Caste-wise break-up of self-help groups during the year 2009-10

Sl.No.	Category	No. of Groups	Percentage
1.	SC	16	32
2.	ST	14	28
3.	BC	05	10
4.	Minorities	04	08
5.	OC	06	12
6.	Others	05	10
	Total	**50**	**100**

Source: Ibid

Among the different castes, SC community belonging to self-help groups are large in number (32%) followed by ST and BC.

The information with regard to activity-wise self-help groups is portrayed in Table 7.6.

Table 7.6: Activity-wise break-up of self-help groups

Sl.No.	Activity	No. of Groups	Percentage
1.	Sheep rearing	20	40
2.	Milk dairy	10	20
3.	Weaving	10	20
4.	Basket Making	05	10
5.	Others	05	10
	Total	**50**	**100**

Source: Ibid.

Among different activities sheep rearing, milk dairy and weaving are the major activities of self-help groups in the district.

PROBLEMS OF WOMEN ENTREPRENEURS

The major problems that are encountered by women entrepreneurs in the district are discussed briefly:

- Finance is regarded as 'life-blood' for any enterprise, be it big or small. However, women entrepreneurs suffer from shortage of finance on two counts. Firstly, women do not generally have property on their names to use them as collateral for obtaining funds from external sources. Thus, their access to the external sources of funds is limited. Secondly, the banks also consider women less credit-worthy and discourage women borrowers on the belief that they can at any time leave their business. Given such situation, women entrepreneurs are bound to rely on their own savings, if any, and loans from friends and relatives which are expectedly meager and negligible. Thus, women enterprises fail due to the shortage of finance.
- Most of the women enterprises are plagued by the scarcity of raw-material and necessary inputs. Added, the high prices of raw material, on the one hand, and

getting raw material at the minimum of discount, on the other. The failure of many women co-operatives in 1971 engaged in basket-making is an example how the scarcity of raw material sounds the death-knell of enterprises run by women.

- Women entrepreneurs do not have organizational set-up to pump in a lot of money for canvassing and advertisement. Thus, they have to face a stiff competition for marketing their products with both organized sector and their male counterparts. Such a competition ultimately results in the liquidation of women enterprises.
- Unlike men, women mobility in India is highly limited due to various reasons. A single woman asking for room is still looked upon suspicion. Cumbersome exercise involved in starting an enterprise coupled with the officials humiliating attitude.
- In India, it is mainly a woman's duty to look after the children and other members of the family. Man plays a secondary role only. In case of married women, she has to strike a fine balance between her business and family. Her total involvement in of husbands seem necessary condition for women's entry into business. Accordingly, the educational level and family background of husbands positively influence women's entry into business activities.
- In India, around three-fifths (60%) of women are still illiterate. Illiteracy is the root cause of socio-economic problems. Due to the lack of education and that too qualitative education, women are not aware of business, technology and market knowledge. Also, lack of education causes low achievement motivation among women. Thus, lack of education creates problems for women in the setting up and running of business enterprises.
- Male domination is still the order of the day in India. The Constitution of India speaks of equality between sexes. But, in practice, women are looked upon as abla, *i.e.,* weak in all respects. Women suffer from male

reservations about a woman's role, ability and capacity and are treated accordingly. In nutshell, in the male dominated Indian society, women are not treated equal to men. This, in turn, serves as a barrier to women entry into business.

- Women in India lead a protected life. They are less educated and economically not self-dependent. All these reduce their ability to bear risk involved in running an enterprise. Risk-bearing is an essential requisite of a successful entrepreneur.
- In addition to above problems, inadequate infrastructural facilities, shortage of power, high cost of production, social attitude, low need for achievement and socio economic constraints also hold the women back from entering into business.

EPILOGUE

To sum up, women plays a stupendous role in the economy. The entrepreneurial skills of women are highly required for vigorous growth of the economy. But due to several socio-economic problems, women are not coming to the forefront. It these problems are solved, no doubt women can contribute distinctly to the economic development of the nation, especially, in case of drought-prone and backwards districts like Kadapa, women role can't be undermined. Their skills and talents must be exploited properly, so that the backward regions develop well in all respects. Hence, there is a dire need to sole women problems with concerted efforts and make them omnipotent.

REFERENCES

Gupta, C.B. and Khanka, S.S., Entrepreneurship and Small Business Magnet Sultan Chand and Sons, Delhi, 1996.

Vasant Desai, Entrepreneurial Developed (Vol. 3), Himalaya Publishing House, 2008.

Khanka, S.S., Women Entrepreneurship in India, *Journal of Anam University*, Vol. 3(1); January, 1998, pp. 11-16.

www.google.com.

8

Financial Institutional Support to Women Entrepreneurs in India

T. Shobha Rani*
M. Padma Lalitha**

ABSTRACT

Today women had entered into every field. The global evidences buttress that women have been performing exceedingly well in different spheres of activities like academics, politics, administration, social work, sports, space and so on. Now they have started plunging in to industry also, to run the enterprises successfully. They have the zeal to start, has ability to run efficiently and effectively, but the basic problem is lack of awareness about financial support from the institutions, which is the life blood of the enterprises. At this juncture, effective steps are needed to provide entrepreneurial awareness, orientation, skill development programmes and details of financial assistance to women from the institutions, as their functions and opportunities are not popularized much. Hence, this paper concentrates on various financial institutions which provide financial assistance through different schemes to the women entrepreneurs.

* Assistant Professor, Department of Business Administration, AITS, Rajampet, E-mail: sbhsankar8@gmail.com

** Professor and H.O.D., Department of EEE, AITS, Rajampet, E-mail: padmalalitha_mareddy@yahoo.co.in

INTRODUCTION

Women in India constitute around half the country's population. Hence they are regarded as 'Better-half of the society'. In the official proclamation, they are at par with men, but in real life the truth prevails otherwise. Our society is male dominated and women are not treated as equal partners both inside and outside of four walls of the house.. Women entry into business entrepreneurship is traced out as an extension of their kitchen activities mainly to 3 P's *viz.* Pickles, Powder and Papad. Now women status is shifting from 3 P's to 3 E's *i.e.* Engineering, Electronics and Energy.

The Indian economy has been witnessing a drastic change since mid 1991, with new policies of economic liberalization, globalization and privatization initiated by the Indian government. In India, though women have played a key role in the society, their entrepreneurial ability has not been properly tapped due to the lower status of women in the society. It is only from the Fifth Five-year Plan (1974-78) onwards that their role has been explicitly recognised with a marked shift in the approach from women welfare to women development and empowerment. The development of women entrepreneurship has become an important aspect of our plan priorities. Several policies and Programmes are being implemented for the development of women entrepreneurship in India.

In the words of president APJ Abdul Kalam "Empowering women is a prerequisite for creating a good nation. When women are empowered, society with stability is assured. Empowerment of women is essential as their thoughts and their value systems lead to the development of a good family, good society and ultimately a good nation".

INITIATION TAKEN BY INDIAN GOVERNMENT

In 1986, a National Level Standing Committee on women entrepreneurs was constituted comprising women entrepreneurs and representatives from FICCI, FASSI and NAYE. The committee aimed at providing fiscal and financial incentives including marketing, training and publicity.

A sub committee was then formed which put forwarded the following recommendations for the promotion of women entrepreneurs:

- Designation of lead banks in each state and earmarking funds for women's enterprise development.
- Coordination between various central departments for funding infrastructure development and survey work opportunities.
- Incentives for SSIs employing 50 per cent women workers.
- Publicity and dissemination of information, programmes and policies pertaining to women's enterprise.

The catalyst for women entrepreneurs was the Seventh Five-year Plan which highlighted empowerment and equality for women. The Eighth Five-year Plan (1992-97) recognises that women form nearly half of the population and must therefore be a target group in the promotion of opportunities for self-employment and creation of ways for employment. The National Commission for Women (NCW) was set up in January 1992 with Jayanti Patnaik as the Chairperson.

VARIOUS FINANCIAL INSTITUTIONS

The potential for women to be entrepreneurs has been recognised and encouraged through various institutions which are established to give momentum to the emergence and growth of women entrepreneurs. Figure 8.1 shows classification of various institutions of India.

Financial Institutions

In financial economics, a financial institution is an institution that provides financial services for its clients or members. Probably the most important financial service provided by financial institutions is acting as financial intermediaries. Most financial institutions are highly regulated by government.

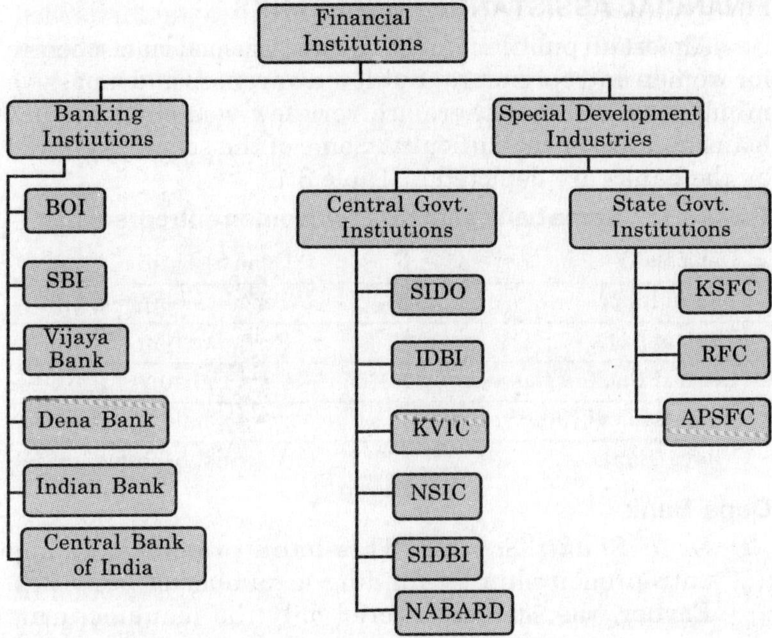

Fig. 8.1: Various Financial Institutions for Women Entrepreneurs

Banking Institutions

An organization, usually a corporation, chartered by a state or federal government, which does most or all of the following: receives demand deposits and time deposits, honors instruments drawn on them, and pays interest on them; discounts notes, makes loans, and invests in securities; collects checks, drafts, and notes; certifies depositor's checks; and issues drafts and cashier's checks.

Development Institutions

Development banks are those financial institutions engaged in the promotion and development of industry, agriculture and other key sectors. These institutions can be classified as central government and state government institutions.

FINANCIAL ASSISTANCE FROM BANKS

Almost all public sector banks have special loan schemes for women entrepreneurs. But low awareness and a passive mindset ensure that there are very few women to acquire loans because of the difficulty. Some of the schemes offered by the banks are depicted in Table 8.1.

Table 8.1: Some bank schemes for women entrepreneurs

Dena Bank	Dena Shakthi
Indian Bank	Term Loan Scheme
Bank of India	Priyadarshini Yojana
Central Bank of India	Cent Kalyani
State Bank of India	Stree Shakti Package
Vijaya Bank	Aravind, Mahima

Dena Bank

(i) *Dena Shakti Scheme*: This bank promotes women entrepreneurship by funding a number of activities. Earlier, the scheme covered only the manufacturing sector, but now has been extended to agriculture and allied activities, small enterprises, micro and small (manufacturing and service) enterprises, retail trade, micro-credit, education and housing.

Dena Bank gives a concession of 0.25 per cent on interest rate. "The maximum ceiling limits that can be considered for financing to women beneficiaries under this scheme will be as per the directives of RBI stipulated for various sectors under priority sector such as loans up to Rs. 20 lakh under retail trade, Rs. 20 lakh under education and housing and Rs. 50,000 under micro-credit as well as the bank's specific schemes circulated to branches/offices from time to time." Considering the fact that a bank has to disburse 5 per cent of the previous year's adjusted net bank credit (ANBC) to women under all schemes.

Indian Bank

Indian Bank was one of the first nationalized banks to open a 'Women's Cell' for potential entrepreneurs. This cell acts as a counselling unit for women who wish to undertake entrepreneurial activity. It also acts as an intermediary between the bank and the beneficiary. This cell also provides information pertaining to training, products and loans available to women.

A loan amount up to Rs. 6,000 per beneficiary at 4 per cent interest The loan is given under the scheme of assistance to urban poor women for self-employment purposes and a term loan (SSI) scheme for women entrepreneurs with 1 per cent rate of interest.

Bank of India

The Priyadarshini Scheme of the Bank of India provides long-term and working capital assistance under the following categories:

- To the professional and self-employed, *e.g.*, chartered accountants, lawyers and doctors.
- To small businesses *e.g.*, beauty parlours, laundries and circulating libraries.
- To retail traders *e.g.*, fair price shops, general provision stores.
- To village or cottage and small-scale industries.
- To road transport operators *e.g.*, auto-rickshaws or taxi drivers.
- For allied agricultural activity.

The maximum loan amount sanctioned depends on the entrepreneur's needs, with limits of up to Rs. 2 lakhs for term loans and up to Rs. 1 lakh for working capital. Interest rates depend up to quantum of the loan. Repayment schedules are fixed after taking into account the expected surplus income, and normally span a period of three to five years. The assets acquired with bank finance have to be hypothecated to the bank as security. The entrepreneur's contribution margin is about 20 per cent, depending upon the type of activity he/she intends to undertake.

For example, under the Priyadarshini scheme of the Bank of India (BOI), the concession on rate of interest varies from 0.25 per cent to 0.50 per cent on retail banking that includes several loans like personal loans.

State Bank of India

The State Bank of India has introduced a programme called the 'Stree Shakti Package' for financial enterprises set up by women entrepreneurs. An enterprise where the woman holds a minimum financial interest of 51 per cent of the share capital and gives at least 50 per cent of the employment generated. Women, is eligible for assistance under this package.

Central Bank of India

(i) *Cent Kalyani Scheme:* This is a scheme launched to benefit women entrepreneurs and women professionals. This scheme offer financial assistance for economic pursuits in Industry, Agricultural and Allied Activities, Business or Profession. The Bank with a network of branches spread throughout the country welcomes women entrepreneurs to avail financial assistance for pursuing vocations of their choice.

Credit facilities are available for Women Entrepreneurs for the following:

- *Small Business*: For entrepreneurs who intend to provide service (not a professional service) such as setting up a small lunch/canteen, mobile restaurant, circulating library etc.
- *Professional and Self-employed:* Entrepreneurs who are specially qualified/skilled and experienced like Doctors, Chartered Accountants and Engineers or trained in Art or Craft etc.
- *Retail Trade*: For entrepreneurs who intend to engage in retail trading of various commodities.
- *Village and Cottage / Tiny Industries:* For entrepreneurs who are engaged in manufacturing, processing, preservation and services such as Handloom, Weaving Handicraft, Food-Processing, Garment making etc. In village and small towns with a population not exceeding 50,000 utilising locally available resources/skills.
- *Small-scale Industries*: To start a unit engaged in manufacture, processing or preservation of goods.

- *Agriculture and Allied Activities*: For women entrepreneurs who are engaged/intend to engage in agricultural and allied activities, such as raising of crops, floriculture, fisheries, bee-keeping, nursery, sericulture etc., and also trading in agricultural inputs.
- *Government Sponsored Programmes*: Apart from the above schemes, women entrepreneurs are also financed under the various Government Sponsored Programmes where Capital subsidies are available.

Vijaya Bank

Vijaya Bank is offering two schemes for women entrepreneurs *viz.* 'Arwind' and 'Mahima'.

(i) *Assistance to Rural Women in Non-farm Development (ARWIND):* The scheme of Assistance to Rural Women in Non-farm Development (ARWIND) is to support their economic activities in Non-farm sector on a cluster or group basis by rural women. This scheme has two components – Credit Components, Promotional Components.

Under Credit component, a voluntary agency having minimum three years of proven track record in assisting women's groups, women's development corporation set up by the Central or State governments, KVIC/KVIBs or any institutions under the KVIC/KVIB fold, any other registered institution including cooperatives, trusts and corporations set up by Central or State governments for the purpose may evolve a scheme to organize rural women's groups for undertaking any productive activity in the non-farm sector and assist them in setting up their own units and/or provide such other backward or forward linkages including training as are considered necessary for improving viability of individual or group enterprises.

The loan assistance under this scheme to the individuals, would not normally exceed Rs. 50000/- per borrower or say Rs. 10 lakhs for a group activity involving 20 rural women. As per Reserve Bank of India guidelines, for loans upto Rs. 25000/- per borrower, no margin money or collateral security or third party guarantee will be insisted upon by the financing banks except hypothecation of assets created out of the loans. The rate of interest chargeable to the beneficiaries or banks will be those as may be specially by the Reserve Bank of India/NABARD from time to time. Repayable may be subject to the cash flow of the scheme, the loan repayment period will be between 3 to 10 years with a moratorium of 6 to 12 months.

(ii) *Assistance for Marketing of Non-farm Products of Rural Women (MAHIMA):* Assistance for Marketing of Non-farm Products of Rural Women (MAHIMA) scheme envisages providing loan and also assistance in grant to the Registered Voluntary Agencies (VA), Non-governmental Organizations (NGOs) and other promotional organizations engaged in marketing the products of rural women. The organizations should have been working for at least three years with proven track record and experience in production or marketing of rural products and should satisfy the norms of the financing banks and NABARD prescribed from time to time.

CENTRAL GOVERNMENT INSTITUTIONS

There are a variety of specialized central-level organizations which provide different types of support to women involved in economic activities. A few such institutions are profiled below.

Small Industries Development Organization (SIDO)

SIDO was established in 1954 on the basis of the recommendations of the Ford Foundation. This government agency mainly concerned with training programmes for women, and promotion of employment and self-employment (is the Small Industries Development Organization (SIDO) SIDO and its chain of Small Industries Service Institutes (SISI) spread all over the country. The SISI conduct training programmes for women entrepreneurs and actively assist women in setting up their own enterprises. SISI is also popular amongst women entrepreneurs for its continuing education programmes on small enterprise management.

SIDO has established a 'Women's Entrepreneurial Cell'. Women entrepreneurs get special consideration by adding 5 per cent means weightage.

Small Industries Development Bank of India (SIDBI)

Small Industries Development Bank of India (SIDBI) was established in April 1990 under an Act of Indian Parliament as the principal financial institution for Promotion, Financing, Development of industry in the small-scale sector and coordinating the functions of other institutions engaged in similar activities. Since its inception, SIDBI has been assisting the entire spectrum of SSI Sector including the tiny, village and cottage industries through suitable schemes tailored to meet the requirement of setting up of new projects, expansion, diversification, modernization and rehabilitation of existing units.

(i) *Schemes of Assistance for Women Entrepreneurs:* All projects in the SSI sector promoted and managed by women entrepreneurs, including those in the cottage, village and tiny sector industries are eligible for this scheme. SIDBI extended assistance of Rs. 16.8 crore to 1,021 entrepreneurs in 1994-95. The average assistance per project was 1.6 lakh, which is reflective of the fact that the scheme was taken advantage of by women entrepreneurs taking up small projects in the tiny sector.

(ii) *Mahila Udyam Nidhi Scheme:* All new industrial projects in the small-scale sector, as well as service activities set up by women entrepreneurs which are eligible for finance as per SSI norms, are eligible for assistance under the scheme, provided the cost of the project does not exceed Rs. 10 lakhs.

Purpose is to meet gap in equity Eligible Borrowers Women entrepreneurs for setting up new projects in tiny/ small scale sector and rehabilitation of viable sick SSI units. Scheme operated through SFCs/twin function SIDCs/ Scheduled Commercial Banks/Select Urban Co-operative Banks. Cost of Project is not to exceed Rs. 1 million. Soft

Loan limit is 25 per cent of cost of Project subject to a maximum of Rs. 2,50,000 per project. Service charges are 1 per cent p.a. on soft loan.

(iii) *Informal Lending*: Responding to the reality that a vast segment of the rural poor remain outside the reach of the institutional system, and recognising the need for creating and strengthening self-help groups (SHGs) of the poor, SIDBI has started extending support to voluntary organizations with a good track record which are working with special target groups in rural areas.

Assistance carries interest of 9 per cent per annum. Voluntary organizations are required to charge interest at a rate not more than 12 per cent (although this can go up to 15 per cent with the approval of the Governing Body) to the self-help groups.

(iv) *Marketing Fund for Women (MFW)*: The assistance under the Fund is available to women entrepreneurs and organizations involved in marketing of products manufactured by women entrepreneurs to increase their reach, both in domestic and international markets. The eligible borrowers are SSI units managed by women entrepreneurs which are providing support services like internet, trade related information, advertising, marketing research, warehousing, common testing centres, etc. and to enterprises owned and managed by women.

Besides providing financial assistance as mentioned above, SIDBI could also consider, on a selective basis, developmental assistance by way of soft loans/grants for organizing group activities and programmes such as trade fairs, exhibitions, buyer-seller meets, seminars, workshops, training programmes, etc.

Industrial Development Bank of India (IDBI)

Programmes for training and extension services for women entrepreneurs are organized by IDBI through designated/approved agencies independently.

(i) *Scheme for Women Entrepreneurs*: The scheme has been formulated with the twin objectives of:

Providing training and extension services support to women entrepreneurs through a comprehensive package suited to their skills and socio-economic status, and extending financial assistance on concessional terms, to enable them to set up industrial units in the small-scale sector.

(ii) *Mahila Vikas Nidhi (MVN) Scheme*: IDBI had set up a special development fund (Mahila Vikas Nidhi) with an initial allocation of Rs. 3 crores from its Technical Assistance Fund. Assistance by way of grants and soft loans is to be made available from the Nidhi. Registered voluntary organizations which, have a proven track record, well functioning governing body and working exclusively for women's development, are eligible for assistance. Activities which could be supported under this scheme include setting up training-cum-development centres, undertaking skill up-gradation programmes, marketing assistance, management up-gradation, and other such industrial activities which improve the economic Assist under the scheme is toward, one-nine capital expenditure expenses of voluntary agencies can be met out of other sources of funding.

(iii) *Scheme for Re-finance Assistance to Woven Entrepreneurs*: All projects in the SSI Sector (including cottage, village and tiny industries) promoted and managed by women entrepreneurs are eligible for assistance under this scheme. The minimum promoter's contribution has to be 12.5 per cent per annum .cost for units set up category 'A' backward districts, and 15 per cent of the project cost in all other irrespective of location.

National Bank for Agriculture and Rural Development (NABARD)

(i) *NABARD 'Women's Cell'*: NABARD has set up a 'women's cell' at its head office and nodal branches m each regional office so as to pay focused attention to policies pertaining to rural women. Introduced an exclusive scheme of Assistance to Rural Women in the Non-farm Sector (ARW1ND) to meet the credit and support needs of rural women with umbrella support from voluntary agencies, NGOs, WDCs, co-operatives etc.

NABARD will provide 100 per cent refinance for the bank loans and maximum refinance is restricted to Rs. 10 lakh only. The quantum of assistance by way of promotional grant would normally be restricted to Rs. 5000/- per women entrepreneur to be covered by the agency concerned or up to 25 per cent of the minimum sales turnover of Rs. 10 lakh envisaged to be achieved within three years, whichever is lower.

In other words would mean that the promotional grant assistance would normally be limited to Rs. 2.50 lakhs per agency, in case the agency is able to cover a minimum of 50 women individually or in groups, with a turnover of Rs. 10 lakhs in order to make it minimum of 50 women individually or in groups, with a turnover of Rs. 10 lakhs in order to make it operationally viable, at least, over a period of three years.

(ii) *Self-help Groups:* NABARD also launched a pilot project on self-help groups in collaboration with commercial banks, regional rural banks and cooperative banks. As on March 31, 1994, 620 groups had been linked with banks and loan amounts of Rs. 84.20 lakh and refinance of Rs. 45.93 lakh had been extended. Out of these 620 groups, as many as 332 groups were exclusively women.

(iii) *Scheme Covered under Automatic Refinance Facility (ARF):* The following are the loan and financial facilities provided under ARF for various projects:

- Financing for setting up artisan units, tiny cottage and village industries - composite loans.
- Setting up of small-scale industrial units and tiny industries - term/composite loans.
- Refinance assistance for infrastructural and promotional support.
- Financial assistance for project formulation and consultancy services.

- Indirect finance through Cooperative societies - composite loan.
- Financing of ISB component under IRDP and SC/ ST action plan - composite loans.
- Sericulture sector ,Coir sector; Handicrafts sector — term loans.
- Project finance for agro industries — term loans.

The Khadi and Village Industries Commission (KVIC)

The Khadi and Village Industries Commission (KVIC) is a statutory body created by an Act of Parliament (No. 61 of 1956 and as amended by Act No. 12 of 1987). Established in April 1957, it took over the work of the former All India Khadi and Village Industries Board. The broad objectives that the KVIC has set before it are:

The social objective of providing employment, the economic objective of producing saleable articles, and the wider objective of creating self-reliance amongst the poor and building up of a strong rural community spirit.

The National Small Industries Corporation Limited (NSIC)

The National Small Industries Corporation Ltd., an ISO 9001:2000 Company, was established in 1955 by the Government of India with a view to promote, aid and foster the growth of Small Industries in the country. NSIC continues to remain at the forefront of industrial development throughout the country, with it's various programmes and projects, to assist the small scale sector in the country. The Corporation provides integrated Technology, Marketing and Financial support to Small Scale Sector. The Corporation provides help to both potential and existing entrepreneurs through a set of schemes like machinery on hire purchase, internal marketing and export marketing assistance, product export, single point registration scheme, etc. These facilities are not women-specific but the women entrepreneurs do get encouragement to avail of facilities from the schemes.

STATE LEVEL FINANCIAL INSTITUTIONS

Every state in India has a State Financial Corporation.

Karnataka State Financial Corporation (KSFC)

Scheme for Women Entrepreneurs

The objective of the scheme is to encourage women entrepreneurs to establish their own projects in the small scale sector by providing financial assistance. Thus, the Corporation provides financial assistance to women entrepreneurs on special terms and at reduced rates of interest so that they can establish their own industrial units.. The Corporation can provide financial assistance up to Rs. 60 lakhs to public or private limited, companies or to registered cooperative societies, In the case of sole proprietors or partnership con-cerns, this limit is up to Rs. 30 lakhs. Interest rates on term loans vary at different locations of the state. A rebate of 1 per cent is given on prompt payment of installments, which includes the interest and principal amounts. In the case of default however, 1.5 per cent penalty interest is charged. A further 1 per cent interest rebate is applicable to women entrepreneurs if they belong to a scheduled caste, scheduled tribe or other backward caste. The minimum promoter's contribution expected in the project under the scheme is location specific. A liberal security margin is fixed depending upon the merits of each case. Normally, the loan is repayable within a period of eight years, including a moratorium period up to two years.

Rajasthan Financial Corporation Scheme for Women Entrepreneurs

Under this scheme, women entrepreneurs get term loans on low margins. The maximum contribution required to be made in the form of share capital by the entrepreneurs is 10 per cent of the project cost. A nominal service charge of 1 per cent is charged under the scheme. Seed capital assistance of 15 per cent of the project cost is allowed to women entrepreneurs, and loans are sanctioned to artisans, cottage industries and also to industrial units set up in the tiny sector.

Andhra Pradesh State Financial Corporation Scheme for Women Entrepreneurs

The objective of this scheme is to provide financial assistance to women having entrepreneurial traits and who can subscribe to at least 51 per cent of the total equity. The project selected should be a small-scale industry and the woman entrepreneur should be the managing promoter with control. Loans sanctioned by SFC should be used exclusively for acquiring' fixed assets such as land, buildings, plant and machinery items. For units located in notified backward areas, SFC charges 12 per cent interest on the net loan sanctioned, and 12.5 per cent interest for units located in other than notified backward areas.

The promoter's contribution should be at least 15 per cent of the total project cost irrespective of the location, and the debt-equity ratio should be at 3:1 of the total project cost. Loans are sanctioned on mortgage of land and buildings and hypothecation of plant and machinery. In the case of sole proprietary and partnership firms, third party guarantee is not insisted upon, subject to a limit of Rs. 5 lakhs. In the case of private and public limited companies, the term loans should be guaranteed by the directors.

OTHERS

In addition to above institutions, women entrepreneurs are also eligible for financial assistance under the following government sponsored programmes where the capital subsidy is available and the rate of interest is very low:

- Self-employment Scheme for Educated Unemployed Youth (SEEUY).
- Self-employment Programme for the Urban Poor (SEPUP).
- Integrated Rural Development Programme (IRDP).

If the entrepreneur has not received finance under any subsidy linked scheme of the Central/State government, and the annual income does not exceed Rs. 6,400 (in rural areas) and Rs. 7,200 (in semi-urban, and metropolitan areas), she is also eligible for finance under the "Differential Rate of Interest Scheme" at 4 per cent per annum.

CONCLUSION

It can be concluded that though there are many institutions to provide financial assistance to the women entrepreneurs in our country, this facility is not availed by majority of the women entrepreneurs. The reasons behind this are lack of awareness about the institutional schemes and mind set of entrepreneurs who believe that the procedure of sanctioning the loans is cumbersome. It was clearly stated in those schemes that the procedure of application and sanctioning are similar to other loans. So, this opportunity should be availed by women entrepreneurs to the optimal extent, as this assistance is provided with concession in order to encourage and empower women.

REFERENCES

Lalitha Iyer: Women Entrepreneurs – Challenges and Strategies Frederic Exert Sifting (FES), New Delhi.

M. Soundarapandian: Women Entrepreneurship – Issues and Strategies. Edited Volume. Kanishka Publishers, New Delhi.

"Entrepreneurial Development"– By S.S. Khanka, HPH, pp. 40-60.

Rao Padala Shanmukha (2007) "Entrepreneurship Development among Women: A Case Study of Self-help Groups in Srikakulam District, Andhra Pradesh" *The Icfai Journal of Entrepreneurship Development* Vol. 1V, No. 1.

Sharma Sheetal (2006), "Educated Women , Powered, Women" *Yojana* Vol. 50, No. 12.

Shiralashetti A S and Hugar S S "Problem and Prospects of Women Entrepreneurs In North Karnataka District: A Case Study" *The Icfai Journal of Entrepreneurship Development* Vol. 4, No. 2.

Saraswathi S.D., (2004), "Making it Happen: Beyond Theories of the Firm Design." *Entreprencurship Theory and Practice*, 28,6:519-31.

S., Saraswathi S.D., (2005), "Knowing what to do and doing what you know: Effectuation as a Form of Entrepreneur Expertise. *Journal of Private Equity*, 9,1:45-62.

"Think Like A Entrepreneur" – An Article from *Harward Business Review*, Sep, 2010, pp. 55-78.

"Financial Markets and Services' – By Vasant Desai, HPH, pp. 1-20.

9

Women Empowerment through Self-help Groups

Dr. V. Murali Krishna*
Dr. K. Sudarshan**
Dr. G. Purushothamachary***

ABSTRACT

Micro-finance is envisaged as provisioning of financial services to the poor people especially through Self-help Group – Bank Linkage Programme which has received world wide acclaim. To change the fate of poor, socially and economically particularly women, micro-finance has been recognised new welfare programmes and another aim is to provide credit support to the rural poor. The objective of the present study is to analyse the women empowerment through establishing Self-help Group's in Deebaguntla village, Gospadu Mandal, Nandyal Taluka, Andhra Pradesh and also to examine the usefulness of micro-finance in poverty alleviation. Self-help Group's is an innovative way in the development era. It has proven as the best measure to eradicate poverty. Not only it has enhanced the standards of living but also it has empowered women.

* M.Com., M.B.A., Ph.D., Principal I/c, V.R.N. College of Computer Science and Management, Tirupati, A. P.

** M.Com., M.B.A., Ph.D., Department of MBA, Associate Professor, SITAMS-Sreenivasa Institute of Technololgy and Management Studies, Chittoor, A.P.

*** M.Com., M.B.A., Ph.D., Department of MBA, Associate Professor, K.L., University, Vijayawada, A.P.

POVERTY: A BURNING PROBLEM

Poverty is a vicious circle and unbreakable. Primary factors that may lead to poverty include over population, the unequal distribution of resources in the world economy, inability to meet high standards of living and costs of living, inadequate education and employment opportunities, environmental degradation, certain economic and demographic trends, and welfare incentives. Varied aspects to eradicate poverty includes to the topmost priority credit availability to the poor. Poverty is linked in circular chains with population and unemployment. As rural development is the pre-requisite for economic development of the country, the problem lies in the lack of access to the poor to basic services.

In rural areas, the government has undertaken programmes to mitigate the worst effects of adverse monsoon rainfall, which affects not only farmers but village artisans and traders. India has had a number of anti-poverty programmes since the early 1960s like, the National Rural Employment Programme started in the year 1980 from the earlier Food for Work Programme to use unemployed and underemployed workers to build productive community assets. The Rural Landless Employment Guarantee Programme was started in the year 1983 to address the plight of the hard-core rural poor by expanding employment opportunities and building the rural infrastructure as a means of encouraging rapid economic growth. To improve the effectiveness of the National Rural Employment Programme, in 1989 it was combined with the Rural Landless Employment Guarantee Programme and renamed Jawahar Rozgar Yojana, or Jawahar Employment Plan. State Governments are important participants in anti-poverty programmes. To change the fate of poor, socially and economically particularly women, Micro-finance has been recognised new welfare programmes world wide, and another aim is to provide credit support to the rural poor.

MICRO-FINANCE AS A TOOL FOR POVERTY ERADICATION

As Finance is considered as life blood for development. Micro-finance is taking a lead role to meet credit requirements. Micro-finance is emerging as the most viable route to extend financial services to the poor. Micro-finance is envisaged as provisioning of financial services to the poor people especially through Self-help Group – Bank Linkage Programme which has received world wide acclaim. The provision of micro-finance is financial services to the rural and urban poor includes self-employment savings and credit. The activities of micro-finance like technical assistance, small loans. And the larger loans are based on the repayment of the loan receiver's performance. Micro-finance is an aid of development.

Need for Micro-financing

Since independence, various governments in India have experimented with a large number of grant and subsidy based poverty alleviation programmes. These programmes were based on grant/subsidy and the credit linkage was through commercial banks only. As a result, these programmes became unsustainable, perpetuated a dependant status on the beneficiaries and depended ultimately on the Government employees for delivery. This not only led to misuse of both credit and subsidy but banks never looked at it as a profitable and commercial activity as well.

Hence was adopted the concept of micro-credit in India. Success stories in neighboring countries, like Grameen Bank in Bangladesh, Bank Rakiat in Indonesia, Commercial and Industrial Bank in Philippines etc., gave further boost to the concept in India in the 1980s. India thus adopted the similar model of extending credit to the poorest sector and took a no. of steps to promote micro-financing in the country.

Types of Organizations and Composition of the Sector

Micro-finance providers in India can be classified under three broad categories: formal, semi-formal, and informal.

(i) *Formal Sector:* The formal sector comprises of the banks such as NABARD, SIDBI and other regional rural banks (RRBs). They primarily provide credit for assistance in agriculture and micro-enterprise development and primarily target the poor. Their deposits at around Rs. 350 billion and of that, around Rs. 250 billion has been given as advances. They charge an interest of 12-13.5 per cent but if we include the transaction costs (number of visits to banks, compulsory savings and costs incurred for payments to animators/staff/local leaders etc.,) they come out to be as high as 21-24 per cent.

(ii) *Semi-formal Sector:* The majority of institutional micro-finance providers in India are semi-formal organizations broadly referred to as MFIs. Registered under a variety of legal acts, these organizations greatly differ in philosophy, size, and capacity. There are over 500 non-government organizations (NGOs) registered as societies, public trusts, or non-profit companies.

(iii) *Informal Sector*: In addition to friends and family, moneylenders, landlords, and traders constitute the informal sector. While estimates of their importance vary significantly, it is undeniable that they continue to play a significant role in the financial lives of the poor.

MICRO-FINANCE AS BEST ALTERNATIVE

The role of micro-finance is well recognised as most suitable and feasible alternative for growth and poverty alleviation. Micro-finance provides financial services to the poor in order to enable them to raise their living standards. The need for micro-finance in India has arisen due to failure of formal banking system in meeting the credit needs of millions rural and urban people. Micro-finance through Self-help Group's is being focused as an alternative system of credit delivery for the poorest of the poor groups. Micro-finance is a programme for the poor and by the poor to mobilize the savings and use them to meet their financing needs. Creating self employment opportunities is one way of attacking poverty and solving the problems of unemployment. A micro-finance institution is an organization that provides micro-finance services, ranging from small non-profit organizations to large commercial banks.

There are over 24 crore people below the poverty line in the country. The scheme of Micro-credit has been found as an effective instrument for lifting the poor above the level of poverty by providing them increased self-employment opportunities and making them credit worthy. Total requirement of micro-credit in the country has been assessed at Rs. 50,000 crore. Micro-credit programme works through NGO or SHGs and the merit lies in weekly monitoring and refund of installments. The rate of recovery under SIDBI's micro-credit programme is as high as 98 per cent. Though there are various departments and organizations implementing micro-credit schemes in the areas of activity falling under their purview but their total reach is very low it is not more than Rs. 5,000 crore. Thus the existing programmes cater to only 5 to 10 per cent of total requirements and there is considerable scope for expansion of such programmes.

Micro-finance Based Poverty Alleviation Programmes

(i) *Swarn Jayanti Gram Swarozgar Yojana*: The Government of India launched the Swarn jayanti Gram Swarozgar Yojana in 1999 where the major emphasis is on self-help group formation, social mobilization and economic activation through micro credit finance.

(ii) *Intervention of NABARD:* Simultaneously, the government supports NABARD, to take up activities such as group formation, micro-finance and economic activation.

Rashtriya Mahila Kosh is a national credit fund for women and the department of women and child development have their own programmes under which micro-credit is being provided for the economic empowerment of the rural poor.

(iii) *Self-help Group – Bank Linkage Programme*: With the growing importance of the micro-credit through SHG bank linkage in India, the Reserve Bank of India in 1996 included 'Financing to SHGs' as a mainstream activity of banks under their priority sector lending.

Micro–finance based Poverty Alleviation Programme

Self-help Group – Bank Linkage Programme: With the growing importance of the micro-credit through Self-help Group bank linkage in India, the Reserve Bank of India in 1996 included 'Financing to Self-help Groups' as a mainstream activity of banks under their priority sector lending.

Role of Self-help Group's

Self-help Groups represent an opportunity for social action and empowerment through women's involvement in considering, addressing and participating in issues that affect their members and their communities, including issues that affect women in particular.

Self-help Groups are a small group of 10-20 individual members in a village who voluntarily come together, and form a group for achieving a common objective. Self-help Groups are small in size with homogeneous membership, and have certain pre-group binding factors.

The individual Self-help Groups are federated into a village organization. The Self-help Group federations provide a forum for regular interaction between Self-help Groups; and help in cross learning's, information dissemination among Self-help Groups, strengthening of primary groups through capacity building, etc. The federation provide essential services to Self-help Groups such as book keeping, audit, training of the Self-help Group members, providing micro-insurance, marketing facilities etc.

A typical village organization may contain 10-30 Self-help Groups in the village. One or two representatives from each Self-help Group are selected for becoming members of the V.O., all the members of the affiliated Self-help Groups constitute the General Body. The Mandal Samakhya is a federation of Self-help Groups at the Mandal level.

Review of Literature

Krakar in his study analysed that as the programme was effectively implemented, the monthly income of the beneficiaries had increased substantially. All the groups had reduced the dependence on money lenders. The major findings of this study revealed that the urge for literacy especially for the girl child and adoption of family planning measures had increased. Self-help Groups had also resulted in improving their standards of hygiene and nutrition. Amal Mandal in his research paper examines the importance of Self-help Groups in poverty alleviation as the groups are organized on the basis of self-help and mutual help. The author viewed that self-help and mutual help may facilitate the sustainable development of women and also views that the group approach is only the way to meet the financial needs through thrift and inter-loaning. Manas Pandey expressed Micro finance through Self-help Groups is an alternative system of credit delivery for the poorest of the poor groups. Micro-finance is a programme for the poor by mobilizing the savings of poor and using them to meet their financing needs.

NEED FOR THE STUDY

Rural people are poor and uneducated. They even have lack of access to minimum basic needs like medical, educated and financial sectors. Though government has emerged out various tools as outcome of poverty in the form of micro-financial institutions. There are some who are unaware of these facilities. And even if they know, they don't show interest to get accessed to. And further more for every service provided there is a loophole, actually the services may not be reachable to the poor. The need of the study is that all these aspects whether these services are reachable to people or not and also to find out the satisfaction levels of the group members.

OBJECTIVES OF THE STUDY

The objective of the present is to analyse to analyse the women empowerment through establishing Self-help Group's in Deebaguntla village, Gospadu Mandal, Nandyal Taluka, Andhra Pradesh and also to examine the usefulness of micro finance in poverty alleviation.

METHODOLOGY

The data for the study were collected through in-depth interviews with the members of the groups, groups leaders and village officer and through observations in Deebaguntla village. The scope of the study is limited to the Deebaguntla village, Gospadu Mandal, Nandyal Taluka, Andhra Pradesh and the Self-help Groups present in that village.

Working of Self-help Group's in Deebaguntla Village

Deebaguntla is a village with 4676 population which consists of 1890 females. The literacy level of the village is 58 per cent. According to community wise categorization BC occupies 38 per cent, SC with 30 per cent, OC with 25 per cent and minorities and SC with a per cent of 7 in the village. The main occupation of the village is agriculture and daily labour.

Gospadu Mandal, Nandyal Taluka, Deebaguntla village consists of 68 Self-help Group's. In each Self-help Group there are 10 to 15 members and every group has two leaders as first and second. The group members are from under poverty line, basically comprise daily wage landless labourers, unorganized sector employees, marginal farmers, urban slum dwellers etc., The members should belong to one region or one area or one community. At first, the group members have to pay Rs. 50 for 6 months as savings. Of considering their promptness in savings if there is no due then only the concerned bank sanctions a loan of Rs. 50,000 to the entire group. After receiving the loan, also the members has to continue to pay Rs. 50 as for savings and repayment of loan amount in monthly installment. Members are at their wish to repay their loan amount. Probably they choose very less duration *i.e.,* 10 months.

The whole village is under Self-help Group – Bank Linkage Scheme with Andhra Pragathi Grameena Bank, Deeba guntla village. After few months the Rs. 50 will pool up and this amount also can be sanctioned to members as loan with interest. In this village, entire 68 Self-help Group's formed into a federation as 'Vijaya Grama Ikya Sangam'.

Entirely 22 villages in Gospadu Mandal and every village have formed as a federation. In the preliminary stage of Vijaya Grama Ikya Sangam only 20 Self-help Group's were there, which were increased to 70 but at present the number of Self-help Groups is 68 as due to default in payment of dues, 2 Self-help Groups were not in form.

President, vice president, secretary, joint secretary and treasurer look after at their official. The official bearers belong to one of the group. The coordination and supervision is done by a village officer – Bharati Reddy.

The relaxation of age is 18-40 years. In the preliminary period, there was no rule of age limit, even 50 years women also eligible to be a member. Unmarried women are not eligible to become a member of Self-help Groups, the reason to say that if they get married, drop-outs may subsist. The federation also sanctions loans to the members of Self-help Group's. They have to attend to the meetings which were arranged by the federation every month on 7th and on 21st. The group leaders will pay their group dues in these meetings and later the paid amount repay to the Mandal office by the federation.

Records for the Awareness of Financial Transactions

Book keeper plays vital role in maintaining or writing records such as minutes, cash book, loan ledger, individual ledger. The records have to be written in the meetings only as to have transparency. A member in the group will be selected as book keeper from the group if she is educated. They are trained for three days. The book keeper is paid with remuneration; it depends upon the age of the group. Older groups have to pay more as the paper work will be more. All members understand all the operations and documents of savings and credit linkage.

End use of Loan

Loan is used to purchase buffaloes, goats. Some people use it for agriculture, for petty shops, kirana shops, tea hotels, vegetable vendors, flower vendors, tailoring, sarees business, chicken supply, poultry. Some people purchased auto rickshaw. Some used in preparing papad, pickles, and in beedi making. Few women took loan for children education and marriage.

OBSERVATIONS MADE

- Money lenders are eliminated by Self-help Groups in the village.
- Self-help Group's surveyed consists of only women.

Categorization of Self-help Groups

While taking into consideration the caste categorization, approx 19 per cent of total groups are OC, 43 per cent of the groups belongs to backward castes, whereas 4 per cent of them are from minorities and 28 per cent of them contribute to form such Self-help Group's belonging to scheduled castes. Even few groups exist in combination of OC and BC but they range only up to 6 per cent.

Size of Groups

It is found that size of groups differs depending upon the number of members present in their group. Among the total groups present in the village, 9 per cent of the groups have 10 members, 7 per cent have 11 members, 24 per cent have 12 members, 21 per cent 13 have members in their group whereas 7 per cent have 14 members and 32 per cent have 15 members in their group.

Age of the Group

Another observation made in the concerned village is the formation of group is some have crossed a decade from the time of formation. There are nearly 10-15 groups that were formed before 2000. Remaining groups were formed only after millennium and that too after forming into federation as Vijaya Ikya Sangam in 2009, up to 18 Self-help Group's were formed in the same year. There are also 2-3 groups which have not yet completed a year from the time of their formation.

Age of the Members

Age of members mostly ranges from 18-50. Some groups consists of even women aged above 50 for whom the government is paying pension of Rs. 500 per month under the scheme of 'Abaya Hastham'. In this village totally 38 members are availing this opportunity. In effect of this the government has prescribed the age limit as between 18 to 40 only.

Literacy Levels

The educational background among Self-help Group members is very low. It is observed that 60 per cent of the members are illiterates, 20 per cent have completed their primary education whereas the other 20 per cent with secondary level education.

Better Relations

All groups have better relations with the other groups and also with Bank officials. They take up many social activities: Cooperation between group members can be seen, as they distribute fund depending on need based. All members are very happy with the Self-help Group's because without any assets or surety they can get loan which are utilised for their economic activities. Domestic violence has diminished as men realized the importance and value their contributions to the house hold. This shows the changes in women role. All women are very confident as they are ready to provide support to their family members in situations where their husbands are helpless. Self-help Group members play a major role in decision-making in their family. Members of every group send their children to schools. Many of them prefer private schools. This shows that they are financially strong enough. Self-help Group's registered a robust growth, both in terms of coverage and the outreach of credit to the poor.

Skills Enhanced: self-help groups have facilitated people learn to work together, they also learned to approach the bank and speak to the visitors.

Attendance at the Meeting: Every Self-help Group conducts meetings regularly on fixed date, time and place, generally all the members should be present if anyone absent, they have to pay Rs. 5 as fine and the meeting goes on in the presence of group leaders. As in the day time all members are busy with their work they fix meetings in the evening. Usually the meeting will be on one day before their payment of dues.

Fund collections from members, financial decisions and disbursements of loans to members are major discussions. The association of members with Self-help Group's had enriched them and enhanced their income earning capacity. The members belonging to SC groups are given an acre of land which costs to Rs. 92000. Out of which Rs. 52000 is paid by government, only remaining 40,000 is to be paid by the member as Rs. 2000 per year. And the land has registered with the member's name. In the village 76 SC members has got land and have registered. As SC people are given more preference. The federation Vijaya Ikya Sangam provides loan for preliminary needs to harvest like fertilizers, seeds and to purchase implements. By this scheme a landless person has become an owner of an acre land which can be harvested twice in a year. Self-help Group's member husbands are covered under Indra Jeevitha bema (Aam Aadmi). For which he has to fill an application and pay Rs. 15. This scheme insurers the person, if he met an accident, he will be paid Rs. 35,000 to cover hospital charges. If the registered person dies an accidental death his family is paid Rs. 75000 or else a natural death occurs his family is paid with Rs. 30,000. This scheme applies for a year only. For the next year it should get renewable by paying Rs. 15. If a person die's under this scheme his children are paid scholarship of Rs. 100 per month.

Repayment of Loan: payment of interest and repayment of principal over the loan will be decided by Self-help Group which will be in fixed installments that are monthly. It is observed that repayment of loan among group members is cent per cent. Self-help Group borrowing implies that all members of a group are responsible for ensuring loan repayments. If any defaulter exists in the group, the defaulter has to pay with fine in the next installment, but the group members are not in a position to adjust their savings towards the defaulter. These shows the earnings are self-sufficient.

Appraisal of the Groups: Depending upon their repayments of dues, conduct of meetings, attendance of members in meetings, regularity of savings, maintenance of records Self-help Group's are given grading. Out of 70 group most of the Self-help Group's are given 'A' grade. Few groups with few defaults are given 'B' grade. Out of 70 Self-help Groups 2 groups are not in form because of defaulters. Now exist only 68 groups in Deebaguntla village.

About Group Leaders: Group leaders are confident, intelligent, solves problems, courageous, sociable and willing to learn. Every lady is interested to be a member but not as a leader. As a leader has to perform number of duties and has to be responsible for many things. Like arranging meetings, payment of dues. This was the major problem faced by the groups, but now they found solution to this problem as every member by turn acts as a leader, presides the meeting, look after the repayments of dues and performs her duties well. Many times clashes occur between the members as to allocation of the loan. This arises because two or more members demands at the same time. This is solved by the urgency and intensity of requirement or both have shared the loan amount. The women in the village never go out of their houses. Now with their family members support as they are going to attend meeting, in paying the deposits. With this we can say that there is definitely an improvement in their life style. Self-help Groups have empowered the members which increased their self confidence to guide their own destinies. In the village LPG gas stove were distributed to Self-help Group's members at Rs. 1500, which cost to Rs. 8000 in the market. It is observed that among all groups only few members are educated that to up to 10 class. Many of them are uneducated even group leaders are found uneducated. NABARD has visited the village to train the rural people in candle making, paper plate's preparation but after that they never addressed. Self-help Group's members are busy with satisfying their needs. They never interacted with any social issues like alcoholism and dowry problem. When any evils occur at that they react. Actually they lack social awareness, but they are ready to take up such activities.

Some times bank officers never cooperate. For a question about savings: Many people expressed the same view. That every woman has left with no savings because they have to repay due to bank, if they took loan from federation it also to be repaid and monthly savings in bank Rs. 50 again they have to look after domestic needs. So members find hard to save. Few members agree that their earnings are insufficient to meet their needs. They also agree that they have to work hard to pay all dues and the same time the prices of food items have raised they are unable to lead a peaceful life.

SUGGESTIONS

1. Promotion of education among groups is a must.
2. Creating awareness about new economic activities like running a canteen by group members or taking up catering services.
3. Creating awareness about social problems.
4. Giving training in finance related aspects.
5. Awareness has to be created among poor so that they can avail themselves of these services.
6. Government officials and NGOs have to show more interest in motivating and helping the poor to organize themselves into self-help groups.
7. Even media have a role to play in propagating the concept of self-help groups.

CONCLUSION

Self-help Group's is an innovative way in the development era. It has proven as the best measure to eradicate poverty. Not only it has enhanced the standards of living but also it has empowered women. Just as we turn the coin Self-help Group's have turned the fate of women. It has given high levels of satisfaction to all. Micro-finance though is not a miracle in the hands of magician to change the fate of poor but gradually by the lapse of time it would show its results in the route of development.

REFERENCES

Karkar., 'Andhra Women March to Wards Empowerment', Gramin Vikas, Vol. 11(4), 1995.

Amal Mandal., 'Swarnajayanthi Gram Swarozgar Yojana and Self-help Group An Assessment', *Kurukshetra*, Jan. 2005.

Manas Pandey, 'Micro-finance: An Instrument for Poverty Alleviation: A Study on Eastern Uttar Pradesh in India", *The Indian Journal of Commerce*, April-June 2009.

S. Rajesh, G. Venkatamma, "Micro-finance Institutions in India", *Kurukshetra*, Nov. 2009, pp. 11-13.

Dr. Shankar Chatterjee, "Rural Employment Programmes Fuelling Development of Indian Economy", *Kurushetra*, Oct. 2009, p. 26.

M.S. Gupta, "Micro-finance Through Self-help Groups – An Emerging Horizon for Rural Development", *The Indian Journal of Commerce*, July-Sep 08, pp. 48-52.

Manas Pandey, "Micro-financing: A Blessing for the Poor", *The Indian Journal of Commerce*, July-Sep 08, pp. 48-52

Dr. B.K. Swain, 'Social Empowerment of Rural Mass Through Self-help Group's', Professional Banker, Icfai University Press, Feb. 08, pp. 49-52.

http://www.edarural.com/documents/Self-help Group-Study/Executive-Summary.pdf

www.nabard.org/pdf/report_financial/Chap_VII.pdf

10

Role of Indian Women in Entrepreneurship

Radharani Kothakalla*

ABSTRACT

The Indian economy has been witnessing a drastic change since mid-1991, with new policies of economic liberalization, globalization and privatization initiated by the Indian government. India has great entrepreneurial potential. Our paper assesses the role of Indian women in Indian entrepreneurship.

INTRODUCTION

The word ' entrepreneur' derives from the French word 'Entreprendre' (to undertake). In the early 16th Century it was applied to persons engaged in military expeditions, and extend to cover construction and civil engineering activities in the 17th century, but during the 18th century , the word 'entrepreneur' was used to refer to economic activities. Many authors have defined 'entrepreneur' differently. Generally, an entrepreneur is a person who combines capital and labour for production. According to Cantillion "entrepreneur is the agent who buys means of production at certain prices, in

* Research Scholar, Department of Commerce, Osmania University, Hyderabad.

order to sell at prices that are certain at the moment at which he commits himself to his cost". According to P.F Drucker "he is one who always:

1. Searches for change,
2. Responds to it,
3. Exploits it as an opportunity."

CONCEPT OF WOMEN ENTREPRENEUR ENTERPRISE

A small-scale industrial unit or industry – related service or business enterprise, managed by one or more women entrepreneurs in a concern, in which they will individually or jointly have a share capital of not less than 51 per cent as shareholders of the private limited company, members of co-operative society". In this dynamic world, women entrepreneurs are an important part of the global quest for sustained economic development and social progress. In India, though women have played a key role in the society, their entrepreneurial ability has not been properly tapped due to the lower status of women in the society. It is only from the Fifth Five-year Plan (1974-78) onwards that their role has been explicitly recognized with a marked shift in the approach from women welfare to women development and empowerment.

The development of women entrepreneurship has become an important aspect of our plan priorities. Several policies and programmes are being implemented for the development of women entrepreneurship.

Table 10.1: Women work participation in india from 1970-2001

India	Percentage
1970-71	14.2
1980-81	19.7
1990-91	22.3
2000-01	25.7

Source: www.wcd.nic.in

Table 10.2: Women work participation when compare to other countries in 2001

Country	Percentage
India	25.7
USA	55
UK	53
Indonesia	40
Sri Lanka	35
Brazil	35

Source: www.wcd.nic.in

Table 10.3: Gender wise work participation rate in India

Census Year	Female	Male	Parsons
1981	19.7	52.6	36.7
1991	22.3	51.6	37.5
2001	25.7	51.9	39.3

Source: www.wcd.nic.in

Table 10.4: State wise women entrepreneurship in india

States	No. of Units Registered	No. of Women Entrepreneurs	Percentage
Tamil Nadu	9618	2930	30.36
Uttar Pradesh	7980	3180	39.84
Kerala	5487	2135	38.91
Punjab	4791	1618	33.77
Maharastra	4339	1394	32.12
Gujrat	3872	1538	39.72
Karnatka	3822	1026	26.84
Madhya Pradesh	2967	842	28.38
Other States and UTS	14576	4185	28.71
Total	**57,452**	**18,848**	**32.82**

Source: www.wcd.nic.in

FINDINGS

Women entrepreneurship development is an essential part of human resource development. But from the above details of four Tables the development of women entrepreneurship is very low in India. Entrepreneurship amongst women has been a recent concern. Women have become aware of their existence their rights and their work situation. However, women of middle class are not too eager to alter their role in fear of social backlash. The progress is more visible among upper class families in urban cities.

CONCLUSION

If a women is empowered her competencies towards decision-making will surely influence her there is a need for changing the mindset towards women so as to give equal rights as enshrined in the constitution. The progress towards gender equality is slow and is partly due to the failure to attach money to policy commitments. In the words of president APJ Abdul Kalam "empowering women is a prerequisite for creating a good nation, when women are empowered, society with stability is assured. Empowerment of women is essential as their thoughts and their value systems lead to the development of a good family, good society and ultimately a good nation."

REFERENCES

Sanjkta Mishra (2008), "Women Enterpreneuship Development in India", Global Institute of Management, Bhuvaneswar.

N. Suneetha (2006), "Economic Empowerment of Women through DWCRA Scheme", Ph.D., thesis, Department of Political Science, HCU, 2006.

Rambabu. G., (2008), "Enterprise Promotion and Self-help Groups (SGHs) in Andhra Pradesh" Ph.D., thesis, Department of Commerce, TU, Nizamabad.

2008, Sathiabama K. (2010), Rural Women Empowerment and Entrepreneurship Development" Assess Student Papers, 2010.

D. Jaya Kothaipillai, (1995), Women Empowerment, Gyan Publishing House, New Delhi, 1995.

Agarwal C.M., (2001), Indian Women, India Publishers and Distributors, Delhi.

www. serp.org. in

www. google. com

Department of Rural Development Reports, 2009.

11

Women Entrepreneurship 'Motivation'
A Driving Vigor to Economic Development

K. Venkata Subbaiah*
G.V. Chandra Mouli**
Dr .P. Suresh***

ABSTRACT

The development of women as entrepreneurs will generate multifaceted socio-economic benefit to the country. Participation of women in economic activities is now emerging as a universal phenomenon. In advanced countries of the world, there is a phenomenal increase in the number of self-employed women after the II world war. In USA women owned 26 per cent of the total business in 1980 and it increased to 32 per cent in 1990 and 41 per cent in 2003. In Canada, one-third of small business is owned by women and in France one-fifth of the industries are owned by women. Apart from earning a livelihood and/or making profit, the entrepreneur is also motivated to fulfill his/her innate urge to achieve success in life, improve his/her social standing, gaining social recognition, to

* M.Com., M.B.A., Assistant Professor, Sri Venkateswara Institute of Science and Technology, Kadapa, A.P.

** M.B.A., M.Com., Incharge and Assistant Professor, Global College of Engineering and Technology, Kadapa, A.P.

*** M.Com., Ph.D., H.O.D. and Associate Professor, Global College of Engineering and Technology, Kadapa, A.P.

provide something to society. The motivational factor vary from place to place, time to time as well as entrepreneur to entrepreneur. Yet motivation moulds the different entrepreneurial traits. The traits and motivation are moulded by the socio, economic, political, cultural and psychological environment and varies from country to country. National Alliance of Young Entrepreneurs, National Institute for Entrepreneurship and Small Business Development, National Institute of Small Business Extension Training, Small Industries Development Bank of India are the other agencies rendering assistance to women entrepreneurs." Women entrepreneurs have been making a significant impact in all segments of the economy in Canada, Great Britain, Germany Australia and U.S.A." The present paper aims at studying various entrepreneurial traits and motivational aspects which are useful in developing a profile of a successful Women Entrepreneur. It is indeed a positive approach in developing entrepreneurship and enterprise in the country. Although, the entrepreneurial traits are complex, the goal of entrepreneur is to build enterprises to earn profit and serve the society.

INTRODUCTION

The development of women as entrepreneurs will generate multifaceted socio-economic benefit to the country. Participation of women in economic activities is now emerging as a universal phenomenon. In advanced countries of the world, there is a phenomenal increase in the number of self-employed women after the II world war. In USA women owned 26 per cent of the total business in 1980 and it increased to 32 per cent in 1990 and 41 per cent in 2003. In Canada, one-third of small business is owned by women and in France one-fifth of the industries are owned by women. Apart from earning a livelihood and/or making profit, the entrepreneur is also motivated to fulfill his/her innate urge to achieve success in life, improve his/her social standing, gaining social recognition, to provide something to society.

The motivational factor vary from place to place, time to time as well as entrepreneur to entrepreneur. Yet motivation moulds the different entrepreneurial traits. The traits and motivation are moulded by the socio, economic, political, cultural and psychological environment and varies from country to country. National Alliance of Young Entrepreneurs, National Institute for Entrepreneurship and Small Business Development, National Institute of Small Business Extension Training, Small Industries Development Bank of India are the other agencies rendering assistance to women entrepreneurs. The Government of Tamil Nadu has set up Tamil Nadu Corporation for Development of Women for Development and Empowerment of Women. It is nodal agency for implementation of various projects.

The study of entrepreneurial traits and motivation is useful in developing a profile of a successful entrepreneur. It is indeed a positive approach in developing entrepreneurship and enterprise in the country. Although, the entrepreneurial traits are complex, the goal of entrepreneur is to build enterprises to earn profit and serve the society.

Motivation

Motivation encompasses complex aspects of human behaviour to which contribution has been made by sociologists, social anthropologists, psychologists and business executives. This concept has its roots in motives within a person which induce him to behave in a particular manner. Generally speaking, the concept of motivation is by and large psychological which "relates to those forces operating within the individual employee or subordinate which impel him to act or not to act in certain ways"–

"Motivation refers to the way in which urges, drives, desires, aspirations, strivings or needs direct, control or explain the behaviour of human beings."

This is a deep-seated definition of Motivation. It includes three things:

1. The urges, drives, desires, aspirations, strivings or needs of human beings influence human behaviour.

2. The factors which influence human behaviour – psychological, sociological, economic or managerial.
3. The efficiency of such behaviour – this may be tested by the resultant action. Whether this behaviour has directed, controlled or implemented the desired action.

Motivational factors constitute the inner urge present in an individual which continuously demands from him to do something new and unique as also to perform better than others. The motivational factors again are comprised of three basic elements – entrepreneurial motivation, personal efficiency and coping capability. The achievement motivation is also termed efficiency motivation. McClelland and Winter have made considerable studies and concluded that what motivates a person to do something new or something to seek better is the inner urge which directs him towards such ends. This urge also forces a person to use the resources efficiently than to be negligent of it. Also important is the power of motivation which is really the urge to have control over others and to direct their course of activities towards the end which one seeks to attain. These motivational factors include the person to undertake entrepreneurial activities which relate to creating a new business where there was none. This also means to excel the performance in carrying out any activity by striving through persistent efforts unlike others who do not have sufficient capacity for hard work.

What Makes an Entrepreneur?

This is a frequent question. What makes an entrepreneur is the combination of various factors that have enabled the personality formation right from the childhood as also the psychological urge that exists intensively in the person.

These psychological processes which lead men to set up their own successful business enterprises begin in the very early life and have cumulative effect. The influences of early childhood and other social roles are determinant factors for the formation of that personality which motivates an individual towards becoming an independent businessman or entrepreneur.

In the case of persons who take up jobs, it has always been found that they have secured success in the established organizations. These people do not have a rejection towards the established institutions and neither do they attempt to rebel against the traditional path to success. On the other hand, an entrepreneur fails to achieve educational success through the established organizations and this is because of the general rejection of the established organizations at all levels. People who tend to like security and not uncertainty get more satisfied by taking up jobs which are less risk-oriented and hence are not motivated towards building up their own industrial enterprise.

Since new employees and managers will be of a caliber selected with an eye on the future, they will all be of a high competence level. It will be a challenge to keep motivating them. It is conceivable that organizational structure will have to be looked into order to meet motivational needs of people and 'position' them in jobs with the right type of responsibility.

Introduction of high technology and workgroups operating without the traditional band of supervisors or inspectors will become more common. Such 'semi-autonomous work groups' will have to be trained so that they are motivated to take care of equipment and meet output targets and tough quality standards.

This will also demand leadership attributes of a high order on the part of people manning such decentralized operations.

CONCEPT OF WOMEN ENTREPRENEURS

Women entrepreneurs are the women or group of women who initiate, organize and operate a business enterprise.

The Government of India has defined women entrepreneurs as "an enterprise owned and controlled by a woman having a minimum financial interest of 51 per cent of capital and giving atleast 51 per cent of the employment generated in the enterprise to women."

Women Entrepreneurship : Sources of Supply of Motivation

Author	Entrepreneurial Phenomenon	Source of Entrepreneurial Supply	Motivate Force or Triggering Factor
1. Schumpeter	Individual	Extraordinary individuals	Innate urge to achieve success
2. Weber	Status Groups	Extraordinary individuals	Religious beliefs Calninist ethic
3. McClelland	Religious and Social Groups	Individuals with high achievement, creative	Child-rearing practices and climate
4. Hagen	Subordinated Groups	Individuals in the society driven by a duty to achieve	'Status withdrawal' and 'relative social blockage'
5. Cochran	Individual	Society's model, personality determined by its cultural values, role expectations and social sanctions	'Social Acceptance' of entrepreneurial role
6. Young	Homogenous	Relative sub-groups (ethnic communities) occupational groups, or Politically-oriented factions	Deviant view of the world strengthened by group solidarity
7. Kunkel	Group	Operant conditioning procedures in a society	Reinforcing stimuli and average stimuli
8. Hoselitz	Group	Culturally marginal groups	Gaining social recognition

FACTORS INFLUENCING THE WOMEN ENTREPRENEURS

Several studies reveal that two factors influence the women entrepreneurs in India.

- **Pull Factors**

Pull factors are those which encourage women to become entrepreneurs. These include desire to do something new in life, need for independence, availability of finance, concessions and subsidies.

- **Push Factors**

Push factors are those which compel women to become entrepreneurs. These include unfortunate family circumstances like death of husband or father, financial difficulties, responsibility in the family etc.

Women Entrepreneurs in India

Women entrepreneurship is relatively a recent phenomenon which came into prominence in late the 1970s. Due to the spread of education, favourable government policies towards development of women, entrepreneurship awareness and new kind of avenues, more and more women are venturing as entrepreneurs in all kinds of business, economic and other useful activities.

Women entrepreneurship in India has come a long way from papads and pickles to engineering and electronics. Now-a-days elite women in cities are making a mark in non-conventional fields such as consultancy, garment exporting, interior designing, textile printing, food processing, chemicals, pharmaceuticals etc.

There were 3 lakh women entrepreneurs in India sharing only 11.2 per cent of total entrepreneurs in 1995-96. In case of small-scale industries nearly 8 per cent are run exclusively by women entrepreneurs.

The women entrepreneurs in India can be classified into three categories:

1. Women with adequate education and professional qualification and a majority of them live in cities. Such women entrepreneurs are engaged in medium and large industrial units and non-traditional establishments. They are not confined to commercial activities but venture into fields such as electronics, engineering and services. This class of entrepreneurs is endowed with high drive, creativity and innovation for taking on the challenging role of entrepreneurship.
2. The second category consists of middle class women who have education but lack training. They are mostly engaged in handicrafts and cottage industries and produce low value added items such as knitting, garments, doll and toy making etc. These women have turned entrepreneurs due to pull and push of traditional and changing values.
3. Women take up business enterprise to tide over financial difficulties when responsibility is thrust upon them due to family circumstances. This group of women entrepreneurs are illiterates, financially weak and are engaged mostly in family business such as horticulture, fisheries, nursery, handlooms etc.

Psychosocial Barriers

Although some women entrepreneurs have excelled in their enterprise, the fear of success haunt women in general. Some psychosocial factors impeding the growth of woman entrepreneurship are as follows:

1. Poor self-image of women,
2. Inadequate motivation,
3. Discriminating treatment,
4. Faulty socialization,
5. Role conflict,
6. Cultural values,
7. Lack of courage and self-confidence,
8. Inadequate encouragement,
9. Lack of social acceptance,

10. Unjust social-economic and cultural system,
11. Lack of freedom of expression,
12. Afraid of failures and criticism,
13. Susceptible to negative attitudes,
14. Non-persistent attitude,
15. Low dignity of labour,
16. Lacking in leadership qualities, *i.e.*, planning, organizing, controlling, coordinating and directing.

Three Pillars for Women's Economic Empowerment With reference to Motivation

First, access to economic resources. Micro-finance figures largely in IFAD's portfolio, with women forming about 80 per cent of the borrowers. In all regions in which IFAD operates from Latin America to Asia – micro-finance programmes have increased women's independent income-earning capacity. In Vietnam, IFAD supported a Rural Income Diversification Project and established a Women's Livelihood Fund (WLF) in each of the beneficiary communes to assist women in carrying out activities that they have identified themselves. The fund is used for any activities that will benefit groups of village women, give support to destitute households, schools and short-term vocational training.

Second, access to land. Giving women secure access to land can transform their lives both economically and socially. IFAD finances development projects in some of the poorest rural areas of the world. In these societies in transition, ways have to be found to improve access to land by poorer groups and women within prevailing although changing – customary legal systems. Increasing pressures on land threaten the loss of land rights by the rural poor, women and indigenous women in particular. IFAD has learned that defending and expanding women's rights requires comprehensive action at different levels: information and capacity-building; organization and empowerment measures; legal assistance and advocacy. Several IFAD funded projects have sought to promote women's access to land.

In Ghana, the Upper-East Region Land Conservation and Smallholder Rehabilitation Project (LACOSREP), promoted women's access to land and water, for both irrigation and domestic use. This ran counter to traditional patterns of land use and ownership and posed a threat to the traditional power structure and shared culture. The project staff therefore tried to win over the traditional chiefs, husbands and male leaders to support women's land rights. The project achieved a notable change. Through the support of local authorities and male leaders, women were able to increase their access to irrigated land by obtaining usufruct rights. However, an analysis of water user association (WUA) members' land showed that women's plots were about a quarter of the size of those of the male farmers.

Third, women need access to markets and trade. In Bangladesh, women used to be harassed by male traders, clients and intermediaries when they were trying to sell their products in the market. The Government in partnership with the World Bank, the Asian Development Bank and IFAD recently introduced a policy of setting up women's sections in major markets. Separate sections were created for women sellers and clean and safe public facilities were established. Interestingly, this has led to changes in local attitudes against women sellers.

As these examples show, access is not enough for women unless secure and safe from harassment and violence. Women also need to be aware of their rights and possibilities to fully enjoy the benefits of access, including time. Several conditions need to be created to this end.

The *first* and most important is alleviating women's workload. Women need time saving tools, opportunities and support in their reproductive responsibilities to be able to make full use of their access to economic resources. The strategy in IFAD supported projects emphasizes the importance of finding ways to reduce the time spent by women on the drudgery of household tasks like fetching water and firewood or preparing meals so that they will have more time for education, economic activities, responsibilities in the community, including at decision-making level and leisure. Mobile day care centres have been introduced in IFAD supported projects to enable women to attend literacy classes and enhanced their participation in community activities.

Working in and with groups is an effective means to reach out to women. Natural resource management groups and self-help groups are used both to generate meaningful participation by women, promote and reinforce solidarity and to provide them with a chance to rise out of their traditionally subordinate role. In Nepal, degraded forestlands were leased to groups of women, willing to undertake their rehabilitation in exchange for secure access to the products thereof. Under a 40-year lease agreement, the leasehold groups have exclusive user rights over the products of the rehabilitated forest in the framework of an agreed management plan. Striking results were achieved by the women leaseholders: an impressive rehabilitation of the forest; increase in bio-diversity; increase in availability of fodder, also increase in school attendance of children due to higher family incomes.

Cultural factors such as prejudice based on stereotypes and male resistance are obstacles to women's economic empowerment. The IFAD supported projects are involving both men and women to achieve change from within. In Mauritania, for example, extension worker couples from Morocco were sent across the border to provide training to men and women in the Oasis Development Project. The sending of extension worker couples enabled a culturally sensitive exchange of knowledge between women and men farmers coming from similar ecological and socio-economical environments. It also became a good example of South-South exchange.

To release women from the constraints on mobility that society imposes on them throughout their lives, high school girls should be compulsorily taught to cycle. There is proof that increased mobility contributes immensely to raising confidence levels. An additional measure that may increase mobility and confidence is to compulsorily train girls also in the methods and techniques of self defense.

CONCLUSION

"Women entrepreneurs have been making a significant impact in all segments of the economy in Canada, Great Britain, Germany Australia and U.S.A."

The areas chosen by women are retail trade, restaurants, hotels, education, cultural, cleaning insurance and manufacturing. The Government of India has defined women entrepreneurs based on women participation in equity and employment of a business enterprise. Accordingly, a woman entrepreneur is defined as an enterprise owned and controlled by a woman having a minimum financial interest of 51 per cent of the capital and giving at least 51 per cent of the employment generated in the enterprise to a woman. The recent trend indicates that women entrepreneurs are sensitive to changing socio-economic conditions in the country. They are keen to take advantage of such positive changes. They also want to prove their mettle in dual role of work at home and participation in entrepreneurial activities. It is expected that the negative attitude towards women entrepreneurs by the family and society will fall off in future.

The development of women entrepreneurship in India depends largely on the exploration of rural market. Rural India comprising nearly six lakh odd villages offers a vast scope for women entrepreneurial activities. Several Asian economies have made great strides towards the development of rural enterprises. For instance, the convergence and development of rural township and village enterprises in China has been most spectacular event in her economic reform. India should emulate China in the matter of accelerating entrepreneurial effort in the country.

REFERENCES

Fisher, Thomas and M.S. Sriram ed., 2002, Beyond Micro-credit: Putting Development Back into Micro-finance, New Delhi: Vistaar Publications; Oxford: Oxfam.

Kabeer N. (2001), "Conflicts Over Credit: Re-evaluation the Empowerment Potential of Loans to Women in Rural Bangladesh": World Development, Vol. 29, No. 1.

Mayoux, L. 1998a. Women's Empowerment and Micro-finance Programmes: Approaches, Evidence and Ways Forward. The Open University Working Paper No. 41.

Ackerley, B. (1995), Testing the Tools of Development: Credit Programmes , Loan Involvement and Women's Empowerment. World Development, 26(3), 56-68.

Johnson, S. (1997), Gender and Micro-finance: Guidelines for Best Practice. Action Aid-UK.

Otero, M., and E. E. Rhyne. Editors. (1994), The New World of Micro-enterprise Finance: Building Healthy Financial Institutions for the Poor. London: IT Publications.

Women Entrepreneurship Development Articles by Gordon and Vasant Desai.

12

Women Entrepreneurship Development in India

Dr. N. Gangisetty*
R. Sesha Sailendra**

ABSTRACT

Women entrepreneurship development is an essential part of human resource development. The development of women entrepreneurship is very low in India, especially in the rural areas. Entrepreneurship amongst women has been a recent concern. Women have become aware of their existence their rights and their work situation. However, women of middle class are not too eager to alter their role in fear of social backlash. The progress is more visible among upper class families in urban cities. This paper focuses on women entrepreneur. Any understanding of Indian women, of their identity, and especially of their role taking and breaking new paths, will be incomplete without a walk down the corridors of Indian history where women have lived and

* Associate Professor, Department of Management Studies, Madanapalle Institute of Technology and Science Madanapalle - 517 325 Chittoor District, A.P., E-mail: gangisetty2006@yahoo.co.in

** Assistant Professor, Department of Management Studies, Madanapalle Institute of Technology and Science, Madanapalle - 517 325, Chittoor District, A.P.

internalized various role models. The paper talks about the status of women entrepreneurs and the problems faced by them when they ventured out to carve their own niche in the competitive world of business environment.

INTRODUCTION

The Indian economy has been witnessing a drastic change since mid 1991, with new policies of economic liberalization, globalization and privatization initiated by the Indian government. India has great entrepreneurial potential. At present, women involvement in economic activities is marked by a low work participation rate, excessive concentration in the unorganized sector and employment in less skilled jobs.

Any strategy aimed at economic development will be lop-sided without involving women who constitute half of the world population. Evidence has unequivocally established that entrepreneurial spirit is not a male prerogative. Women entrepreneurship has gained momentum in the last three decades with the increase in the number of women enterprises and their substantive contribution to economic growth. The industrial performance of Asia-Pacific region propelled by Foreign Direct Investment, technological innovations and manufactured exports has brought a wide range of economic and social opportunities to women entrepreneurs.

In this dynamic world, women entrepreneurs are an important part of the global quest for sustained economic development and social progress. In India, though women have played a key role in the society, their entrepreneurial ability has not been properly tapped due to the lower status of women in the society. It is only from the Fifth Five-year Plan (1974-78) onwards that their role has been explicitly recognised with a marked shift in the approach from women welfare to women development and empowerment. The development of women entrepreneurship has become an important aspect of our plan priorities. Several policies and programmes are being implemented for the development of women entrepreneurship in India.

There is a need for changing the mindset towards women so as to give equal rights as enshrined in the constitution. The progress towards gender equality is slow and is partly due to the failure to attach money to policy commitments. In the words of president APJ Abdul Kalam "empowering women is a prerequisite for creating a good nation, when women are empowered, society with stability is assured. Empowerment of women is essential as their thoughts and their value systems lead to the development of a good family, good society and ultimately a good nation."

When a woman is empowered it does not mean that another individual becomes powerless or is having less power. On the contrary, if a women is empowered her competencies towards decision-making will surely influence her family's behaviour.

In advanced countries, there is a phenomenon of increase in the number of self-employed women after the World War II. In USA, women own 25 per cent of all business, even though their sales on an average are less than two-fifths of those of other small business. In Canada, women own one-third of small business and in France it is one-fifth.

Concept of Entrepreneur – The word ' entrepreneur' derives from the French word 'Entreprendre' (to undertake). In the early 16th Century it was applied to persons engaged in military expeditions, and extend to cover construction and civil engineering activities in the 17th century, but during the 18th century , the word 'entrepreneur' was used to refer to economic activities. Many authors have defined 'entrepreneur' differently. Generally, an entrepreneur is a person who combines capital and labour for production. According to Cantillion "entrepreneur is the agent who buys means of production at certain prices, in order to sell at prices that are certain at the moment at which he commits himself to his cost". According to P.F Drucker" he is one who always:

1. Searches for change.
2. Responds to it.
3. Exploits it as an opportunity".

Concept of women Entrepreneur Enterprise" – A small-scale industrial unit or industry – related service or business enterprise, managed by one or more women entrepreneurs in a concern, in which they will individually or jointly have a share capital of not less than 51 per cent as shareholders of the private limited company, members of co-operative society".

Categories of Women Entrepreneurs

1. Women in organized and unorganized sector.
2. Women in traditional and modern industries.
3. Women in urban and rural areas.
4. Women in large scale and small-scale industries.
5. Single women and joint venture.

Categories of Women Entrepreneurs in Practice in India

- **First Category**
  - Established in big cities.
  - Having higher level technical and professional qualifications.
  - Non traditional Items.
  - Sound financial positions.
- **Second Category**
  - Established in cities and towns.
  - Having sufficient education.
  - Both traditional and non traditional items.
  - Undertaking women services-kindergarten, crèches, beauty parlors, health clinic etc.
- **Third Category**
  - Illiterate women.
  - Financially week.
  - Involved in family business such as Agriculture, Horticulture, Animal Husbandry, Dairy.
  - Fisheries, Agro Forestry, Handloom, Power loom etc.

Supportive Measures for Women's Economic Activities and Entrepreneurship

(i) Direct and Indirect Financial Support

- Nationalized banks.
- State finance corporation.
- State industrial development corporation.
- District industries centres.
- Differential rate schemes.
- Mahila Udyug Needhi scheme.
- Small Industries Development Bank of India (SIDBI).
- State Small Industrial Development Corporations (SSIDCs).

(ii) Yojna Schemes and Programmes

- Nehru Rojgar Yojna.
- Jacamar Rojgar Yojna.
- TRYSEM.
- DWACRA.

(iii) Technological Training and Awards

- Stree Shakti Package by SBI.
- Entrepreneurship Development Institute of India.
- Trade Related Entrepreneurship Assistance and Development (TREAD).
- National Institute of Small Business Extension Training (NSIBET).
- Women's University of Mumbai.

(iv) Federations and Associations

- National Alliance of Young Entrepreneurs (NAYE).
- India Council of Women Entrepreneurs, New Delhi.
- Self Employed Women's Association (SEWA).
- Association of Women Entrepreneurs of Karnataka (AWEK).
- World Association of Women Entrepreneurs (WAWE).
- Associated Country Women of the World (ACWW).

Problems of Women Entrepreneurs in India

Women in India are faced many problems to get ahead their life in business. A few problems cane be detailed as:

1. The greatest deterrent to women entrepreneurs is that they are women. A kind of patriarchal – male dominant social order is the building block to them in their way towards business success. Male members think it a big risk financing the ventures run by women.
2. The financial institutions are skeptical about the entrepreneurial abilities of women. The bankers consider women loonies as higher risk than men loonies. The bankers put unrealistic and unreasonable securities to get loan to women entrepreneurs. According to a report by the United Nations Industrial Development Organization (UNIDO), "despite evidence that women's loan repayment rates are higher than men's, women still face more difficulties in obtaining credit," often due to discriminatory attitudes of banks and informal lending groups (UNIDO, 1995b).
3. Entrepreneurs usually require financial assistance of some kind to launch their ventures – be it a formal bank loan or money from a savings account. Women in developing nations have little access to funds, due to the fact that they are concentrated in poor rural communities with few opportunities to borrow money (Starcher, 1996; UNIDO, 1995a). The women entrepreneurs are suffering from inadequate financial resources and working capital. The women entrepreneurs lack access to external funds due to their inability to provide tangible security. Very few women have the tangible property in hand.
4. Women's family obligations also bar them from becoming successful entrepreneurs in both developed and developing nations. "Having primary responsibility for children, home and older dependent family members, few women can devote all their time and energies to their business" (Starcher, 1996, p.. The financial institutions discourage women entrepreneurs on the

belief that they can at any time leave their business and become housewives again. The result is that they are forced to rely on their own savings, and loan from relatives and family friends.

5. Indian women give more emphasis to family ties and relationships. Married women have to make a fine balance between business and home. Moreover the business success is depends on the support the family members extended to women in the business process and management. The interest of the family members is a determinant factor in the realization of women folk business aspirations.
6. Another argument is that women entrepreneurs have low-level management skills. They have to depend on office staffs and intermediaries, to get things done, especially, the marketing and sales side of business. Here there is more probability for business fallacies like the intermediaries take major part of the surplus or profit. Marketing means mobility and confidence in dealing with the external world, both of which women have been discouraged from developing by social conditioning. Even when they are otherwise in control of an enterprise, they often depend on males of the family in this area.
7. The male - female competition is another factor, which develop hurdles to women entrepreneurs in the business management process. Despite the fact that women entrepreneurs are good in keeping their service prompt and delivery in time, due to lack of organizational skills compared to male entrepreneurs women have to face constraints from competition. The confidence to travel across day and night and even different regions and states are less found in women compared to male entrepreneurs. This shows the low level freedom of expression and freedom of mobility of the women entrepreneurs.
8. Knowledge of alternative source of raw materials availability and high negotiation skills are the basic

requirement to run a business. Getting the raw materials from different souse with discount prices is the factor that determines the profit margin. Lack of knowledge of availability of the raw materials and low-level negotiation and bargaining skills are the factors, which affect women entrepreneur's business adventures.

9. Knowledge of latest technological changes, know how, and education level of the person are significant factor that affect business. The literacy rate of women in India is found at low level compared to male population. Many women in developing nations lack the education needed to spur successful entrepreneurship. They are ignorant of new technologies or unskilled in their use, and often unable to do research and gain the necessary training (UNIDO, 1995b, p. 1). Although great advances are being made in technology, many women's illiteracy, structural difficulties, and lack of access to technical training prevent the technology from being beneficial or even available to females ("Women Entrepreneurs in Poorest Countries," 2001). According to The Economist, this lack of knowledge and the continuing treatment of women as second-class citizens keep them in a pervasive cycle of poverty ("The Female Poverty Trap", 2001). The studies indicate that uneducated women don't have the knowledge of measurement and basic accounting.

10. Low-level risk taking attitude is another factor affecting women folk decision to get into business. Low-level education provides low-level self-confidence and self-reliance to the women folk to engage in business, which is continuous risk taking and strategic cession making profession. Investing money, maintaining the operations and ploughing back money for surplus generation requires high risk taking attitude, courage and confidence. Though the risk tolerance ability of the women folk in day-to-day life is high compared to male members, while in business it is found opposite to that.

11. Achievement motivation of the women folk found less compared to male members. The low level of education

and confidence leads to low level achievement and advancement motivation among women folk to engage in business operations and running a business concern.

12. Finally high production cost of some business operations adversely affects the development of women entrepreneurs. The installation of new machineries during expansion of the productive capacity and like similar factors dissuades the women entrepreneurs from venturing into new areas.

How to Develop Women Entrepreneurs?

Right efforts on from all areas are required in the development of women entrepreneurs and their greater participation in the entrepreneurial activities. Following efforts can be taken into account for effective development of women entrepreneurs.

1. Consider women as specific target group for all developmental programmers.
2. Better educational facilities and schemes should be extended to women folk from government part.
3. Adequate training programme on management skills to be provided to women community.
4. Encourage women's participation in decision-making.
5. Vocational training to be extended to women community that enables them to understand the production process and production management.
6. Skill development to be done in women's polytechnics and industrial training institutes. Skills are put to work in training-cum-production workshops.
7. Training on professional competence and leadership skill to be extended to women entrepreneurs.
8. Training and counselling on a large scale of existing women entrepreneurs to remove psychological causes like lack of self-confidence and fear of success.
9. Counseling through the aid of committed NGOs, psychologists, managerial experts and technical

personnel should be provided to existing and emerging women entrepreneurs.

10. Continuous monitoring and improvement of training programmers.
11. Activities in which women are trained should focus on their marketability and profitability.
12. Making provision of marketing and sales assistance from government part.
13. To encourage more passive women entrepreneurs the Women training programme should be organized that taught to recognise her own psychological needs and express them.
14. State finance corporations and financing institutions should permit by statute to extend purely trade related finance to women entrepreneurs.
15. Women's development corporations have to gain access to open-ended financing.
16. The financial institutions should provide more working capital assistance both for small-scale venture and large scale ventures.
17. Making provision of micro credit system and enterprise credit system to the women entrepreneurs at local level.
18. Repeated gender sensitization programmers should be held to train financiers to treat women with dignity and respect as persons in their own right.
19. Infrastructure, in the form of industrial plots and sheds, to set up industries is to be provided by state run agencies.
20. Industrial estates could also provide marketing outlets for the display and sale of products made by women.
21. A Women Entrepreneur's Guidance Cell set up to handle the various problems of women entrepreneurs all over the state.
22. District Industries Centres and Single Window Agencies should make use of assisting women in their trade and business guidance.

23. Programmers for encouraging entrepreneurship among women are to be extended at local level.
24. Training in entrepreneurial attitudes should start at the high school level through well-designed courses, which build confidence through behavioural games.
25. More governmental schemes to motivate women entrepreneurs to engage in small-scale and large-scale business ventures.
26. Involvement of Non Governmental Organizations in women entrepreneurial training programmes and counseling.

CONCLUSION

Entrepreneurship among women, no doubt improves the wealth of the nation in general and of the family in particular. Women today are more willing to take up activities that were once considered the preserve of men, and have proved that they are second to no one with respect to contribution to the growth of the economy. Women entrepreneurship must be moulded properly with entrepreneurial traits and skills to meet the changes in trends, challenges global markets and also be competent enough to sustain and strive for excellence in the entrepreneurial arena.

REFERENCES

Dhameja S. K., (2002), "Women Entrepreneurs: Opportunities, Performance", Problems, Deep Publications Pvt. Ltd., New Delhi, p. 11.

Rajendran N. (2003), "Problems and Prospects of Women Entrepreneurs" SEDME, Vol. 30, No. 4, Dec.

Rao Padala Shanmukha (2007), "Entrepreneurship Development among Women: A Case Study of Self-help Groups in Srikakulam District, Andhra Pradesh" *The Icfai Journal of Entrepreneurship Development,* Vol. IV, No. 1.

Sharma Sheetal (2006), "Educated Women , Powered, Women" *Yojana* Vol. 50, No. 12.

Shiralashetti A.S., and Hugar S. S. "Problem and Prospects of Women Entrepreneurs in North Karnataka District: A Case Study" *The Icfai Journal of Entrepreneurship Development* Vol. IV, No. 2.

13

Entrepreneur – Catalyst for Women Empowerment

A General Perspective

Dr. V. Ramabrahmam*
Dr. G. Haranath**

ABSTRACT

"Women entrepreneur according to Government of India is an entrepreneur, who runs an enterprise owned and controlled by her and having minimum financial interest up to 51 per cent of the capital giving at least 51 per cent of the employment to women". Women entrepreneur is one who initiates, organize and operate a business enterprise. In developing countries like India such Innovations are found less in number when compared with advanced countries. Entrepreneurship is not related to sex of an individual. Women can be as successful entrepreneur as men. The entry women in business is only a recent development in the orthodox, traditional, social and cultural environment of our society. Our society has not allowed women to think independently in the past. But in last decade, economic compulsions have led more and more young girls to take up employment and potential source of women

* Assistant Professor, Department of History and Archaeology, Yogi Vemana University, Kadapa – Y.S.R. District, Kadapa, A.P.

** Assistant Professor, Department of Commerce, Yogi Vemana University, Kadapa – Y.S.R. District, Kadapa, A.P.

entrepreneurship has emerged. The following are some of the reasons for emerging women entrepreneurship. Not finding a job, Unable to work in her house, New challenges and opportunities for self-fulfillment, Proving their innovative skills, Need for additional income. Finally the above reasons clearly indicate that economic compulsions, family responsibilities and desire to enjoy social status compel the women to take up enterprises, it leads to empowerment.

Women entrepreneur according to Government of India is an entrepreneur, who runs an enterprise owned and controlled by her and having minimum financial interest up to 51 per cent of the capital giving at least 51 per cent of the employment to women".

Women entrepreneur is one who initiates, organize and operate a business enterprise. In developing countries like India such Innovations are found less in number when compared with advanced countries. Entrepreneurship is not related to sex of an individual. Women can be as successful entrepreneur as men. The entry women in business is only a recent development in the orthodox, traditional, social and cultural environment of our society. Our society has not allowed women to think independently in the past. But in last decade, economic compulsions have led more and more young girls to take up employment and potential source of women entrepreneurship has emerged. The following are some of the reasons for emerging women entrepreneurship.

Not finding a job, unable to work in her house, new challenges and opportunities for self-fulfillment, proving their innovative skills, need for additional income.

Swami Vivekananda observed that lack of education weekend the self-confidence of majority of women in India. He drew pointed attention of the people towards the fact that self-confidence was more than half of the 'Secret of Success' in life. Women education of the right type which leads to characters, foundation, strengthening of mind, development of the intellect and self-reliance.

According to Rammanohar Lohia, the emancipating of women was the foundation of social revolution, with out this there can be no prosperity. Mahatma Gandhi was a strong advocate of women's rights. His successful call to women to join the national movement served as a catalyst for the wider participation of women in Public affairs.

WOMEN ASSOCIATIONS

1. The international council of women convened its first meeting in Washington in 1888 to advance to women's social, economic and political rights.
2. The founding member's of women Indian Association in 1917 were Mrs. Annie Besant, Mrs. Margaret cousins and Dorothy Jinarajadasa.
3. The National council of women in India was renamed as All India women's organization established in 1925.
4. The eighth session of the Andhradesa constituency conference was held on 17th November 1934 at the Besant Hall, Madanapalle under the presidency of Srimati. G. Durgabai Deshmukh.

INDIAN CONSTITUTION

The constitution of the country provides for equality of opportunities to all citizens irrespective of race, sex, caste and communities. Recently the supreme court has highlighted the right of the women in India to eliminate gender based discrimination particularly in respect of property so as to attain economic empowerment.

National Commission for Women Act, 1990

The Union Government of India under the leadership of V.P. Singh in 1989 felt that the task of the development of women through their empowerment would not be possible in the absence of a commission for women which act as a nodal agency – a watch dog to safeguard the interests of women and advise government on all issues concerning women.

National Policy for the Empowerment of Women, 2001

The National Policy (2001) was formulated with a view to bridging the gap between the goals enunciated in the constitution, legislation, policies, plan, programmes and related mechanisms on the one hand and situational reality of the status of women in India, on the other.

Some of the important features of the policy include their active participation in decision-making including the political process at all levels, adopting a gender perspective to ensure main streaming of women in all developmental processes, as catalysts, participants and recipients.

Empowerment is the most frequently used term in development dialogue to day. It is also the most nebulous and widely interpreted of concepts. It has simultaneously become a tool for analysis, as also an umbrella concept to justify almost every conceivable development intervention. In the world summit for Social Development held at Copenhagen in March 1995, empowerment featured prominently as an objective.

In the context of development empowerment cannot be given to anyone, nor is it a goal that can be reached by an organization or by the state as an institution. It is a process that takes place where in an inequality moves towards becoming an equality. These can range from education, health services, housing livelihoods, employment remuneration etc.

In order to understand how constraints can be reduced, he have to move on to the concept of 'Spaces'. Physical space constitutes a women's access to the physical space of her body of mobility across spaces outside and with in her house. There is however no linear relationship between the expansion of physical/economic/socio-cultural/political spaces and that of mental space. All forms of violence against women, physical and mental, whether at domestic or societal levels, including those arising from customs, traditions or accepted practices shall be dealt with effectively, with a view to eliminating its incidence. A special emphasis will also laid on programmes and measures to deal with trafficking in women and girls.

The second factor that leads to an expansion of mental spaces is information. Information is a very important source of power as well as an instrument. It is again, a source and instrument of empowerment.

Other policy directions are also aimed at women's access to credit for consumption and production through micro-credit mechanism and micro-finance institutions. There are several institutions engaged in conducting entrepreneurship development programmes in India. Small industries development organization was set up at the apex levels to provide technical inputs and guidance to small industries khadi and village industries commission was established to promote village industries.

In 1984, Government of India set up National Institute for Entrepreneurship and Small Business. At the same time IDBI and other financial institutions set up Entrepreneurial Development of India (EDI).

The following are the important institutions which are operating at state level to assist the entrepreneurs are:

1. Small Industries Service Institute.
2. District Industrial Centre.
3. State Finance Corporation.
4. Technical Consultancy Organization.
5. State Small Industries Corporation.
6. State Industries Corporation.
7. Commercial Banks.
8. State Industries Promotion Corporation.

At the National level, the following institutions are helping the entrepreneurs.

1. Small Industries Development Corporation.
2. Industrial Financial Corporation of India.
3. Industrial Development Bank of India.
4. Industrial Credit and Investment Corporation of India.
5. Minerals and Metals Trading Corporation.
6. National Small Scale Industrial Development Corporation.

7. Khadi and Village Industries Centre.
8. National Bank of Agriculture and Rural Development.
9. Small Industries Development Bank of India.
10. Unit Trust of India.
11. Life Insurance Corporation of India.
12. National Institute of Small Industry Extension Training.

PROBLEMS OF WOMEN ENTREPRENEURS

Most of the women entrepreneurs face peculiar problems like literacy, fear of risk, lack of training and experiences, feeling of insecurity, limited purchasing power and competition from male entrepreneurs. Most important problem faced by a women entrepreneurs that they do not get enough support from family members.

Some of the major problems faced by women entrepreneurs are:

1. Paucity of funds.
2. Competition.
3. Exploitation of Middle men.
4. Legal formation in obtaining license.
5. Procurement of Raw-material.
6. Traveling.
7. Family bonding – Children.
8. Traditional and Customs.
9. Risk Bearing.

CONCLUSION

Commercialization and modernization of the economy gradually eliminated many of the avenues of employment to women in agriculture and industries and thus enabled them to find ways of supplementing their family income. As a result of this, a section of urban women have emerged as potential entrepreneurs. This development is of significant importance in the society. It is since the last decade that the women have started emerging on the business scene and some of them have achieved remarkable success too.

Some of the successful women entrepreneurs in India are:

1. Smt. Vimala Pitre – Manufacturer of Surgical equipment.
2. Smt. Manik Vanrekar – Leather Crafts.
3. Smt. Radhanika Pradhan – Plastic Industies.
4. Lastly Smt. Gogate – Drugs etc.

REFERENCES

Chandrababu, B.S., Thilagavathi, L., Women: Her History and her Struggle for Emancipation, Chennai, 2009, p. 27.

Chandrababu, B.S., Thilagavathi, L., *op.cit.*, pp. 286 and 288.

Chandrababu, B.S., Thilagavathi, L., *op.cit.*, pp. 334, 337, 348.

Indus Grover, Deepak Grover (Ed.), Empowerment of Women, pp. 14-17.

Deshmukh – Ranadive Joy, Space for Power, Women's Work and Family Strategies in South and South – East Asia, New Delhi.

Women and Geography Study Group, Geography and Gender: An Introduction to Feminist Geography, Leicester, U.K: Institute of British Geographers.

Sachidananda and Niraj Kumar, "On Women Empowerment: Promise and Performance", The Eastern Anthropologist, Vol. 59, No. 1, Jan-Mar 2006.

14

Women Entrepreneurship
Information and Communication Technologies (ICT)

Dr. B.C. Saraswathy*
Dr. N. Subbanarasaian**

ABSTRACT

ICT (Information and Communication Technologies) has enormous potential as a tool to enhance women's economic, political and social empowerment. Women entrepreneurs in particular can benefit from these to improve their access to information and network and to increase their competitiveness and market outreach of their businesses. In India, from the Fifth Five-year Plan (1974-78) onwards, the role of women has been explicitly recognised with marked shift in the approach of women welfare to women development and empowerment. Women are increasingly entering the domain of business through entrepreneurial activities and commencing their own businesses and contributing to the national economy in India. ICT tools are acting as the major shield to develop business and extend growth beyond the boundaries. The use of ICT increases women capacities to share and access information and

* Reader in Commerce, Government College for Men, Kadapa – 516 004, A.P.

** Reader in Commerce, Government College for Men, Kadapa – 516 004, A.P.

knowledge besides it supports to develop their entrepreneurial business activities and leads to promote women undertakings in broader space. Although great advances are being made in technology, many a woman's illiteracy structural difficulties and lack of access to technical training prevent the technology from being beneficial or even available to females. Therefore, this paper tries to bring the success stories of women entrepreneurs, challenges faced by them and suggests suitable measures for the faster development of women entrepreneurs and use of ICT in India in the impact of globalization and changing patterns of trade and technological revolution.

Across the globe, the role of the women in economic development has been recognised from nineties onwards. Today, entrepreneurship has become an essential movement in many countries and has been accepted in all areas of working in the world of business. Entrepreneurship is sine qua non for the continued dynamism of the modern market economy. Poverty eradication and gender equality are central development goals for the twenty first century. Women economic empowerment which includes the promotion of women's entrepreneurship supports both the goals.

Former President India, APJ Abdul Kalam has stated that:

"Empowering Women is a prerequisite for creating a good nation, when women are empowered, society with stability is assured. Empowerment of women is essential as their thought and their value system leads to the development of good family, good society and ultimately a good nation."

Women entrepreneurship is instrumental to women empowerment. Fourth World Conference on Women which is held at Beijing in 1995 underscored the need to develop women entrepreneurship. The objectives set by the conference are to:

- Increase the participation of women in industry and all other sectors particularly in non-traditional areas, through access to advanced technologies;

- Promote support and strengthen female entrepreneurship development;
- Encourage investment in environmentally safe products and in environmentally sound and productive agricultural, fisheries, commercial and industrial activities and technologies; and
- Strengthening training opportunities for women.

In the review implementation of the Fourth World Conference, which took place in March 2010, highlighted that support to women entrepreneurs working to expand their business should be increased including through greater access to formal financial instruments training and advisory services, access to markets and facilitation of networking and exchanges.

With support extended and initiatives taken by the Governments women entrepreneurial development in different countries a large number of women entrepreneurs emerged. Today, in advanced market economies more than 25 per cent of all businesses are owned by women. The percentage of women entrepreneurs exceeded even more than 35 in the some of the countries like USA, Poland and Switzerland. Lately, entrepreneurship among women in India has been given due consideration for achieving the goals of poverty eradication and sustained economic growth. From Fifth Five-year Plan (1974-78) onwards, the role of the women has been explicitly recognised with marked shift in the approach of women welfare to women development and empowerment. Thus, the development of women entrepreneurship has gained priority in our plans.

The word entrepreneur is derived from the French word 'entrepredre' which means one who undertakes. Various researchers and scholars have defined entrepreneurs in many ways which gives the quality and substance of the entrepreneurs.

Peter Drucker defines entrepreneur as "a person who perceives business opportunities and take advantage of scarce resources and uses them profitably". According to Peter

Drucker perceiving opportunities and employing scarce resources profitably are the main functions of an entrepreneur. According to Weber, "An entrepreneur is a person who organizes, manages and takes risks of a business enterprise."

Joseph Schumpeter defines entrepreneur as " a person who is willing and able to connect a new idea or invention into successful innovation." In Schumpeter words, entrepreneur should be concerned to reform or revolutionize the pattern of products by employing an invention or more generally an untried technological possibility for producing new commodity or producing an old one in a new way, by opening up a new source of supply of materials or a new outlet for production. Entrepreneurship, as defined, essentially consists of doing things that are not generally done in ordinary course of business routine.

Entrepreneurship has been defined in the literature "the catalytic agent in society which sets into motion new enterprises, new combinations of production and exchange."

Coming to the word woman entrepreneur," in larger sense, woman entrepreneur is a person who accepts challenging role to meet her personal needs and becomes economically self-sufficient." A strong desire to do something positive is an inbuilt quality of entrepreneurial woman, who is capable of contributing value for both family and social life.

Technically, a woman entrepreneur is any one who organizes and manages any enterprise, especially a business, usually with considerable initiative and risk. Like a male entrepreneur a woman entrepreneur has many functions. They should explore the prospects of starting new enterprise, undertake risks, introduction of new innovations, coordination, administration and control of business and providing effective leadership in all aspects of business.

Government of India defined woman enterprise as "an enterprise, which is owned and controlled by a woman or a group of women having a minimum financial interest up to 51 per cent of capital and giving at least 51 per cent of employment to women". However, many women entrepreneurs are not agreeing to this definition as this puts a discriminatory condition and demanding that any enterprise set by women should qualify for concessions offered by the Government.

Women in India are increasingly entering the domain of business through entrepreneurial activities, commencing their own businesses and contributing to the national economy. The unique capabilities of women entrepreneurs should be harnessed and incorporated into national development strategies and encouraged from the secondary education level. The combined substance of entrepreneurship and use of information and communication technology will enable to solve the basic problem of impeded growth of women entrepreneur in India. The impact of globalization and changing pattern of trade and evolving technological revolution is calling for the development skills. Unfortunately, women entrepreneurs in rural and semi-urban areas of India do not possess these skills.

ICT (Information and Communication Technologies) has proven to be the most powerful tool for the growth and development of economy. The information and communication technological system has been used to create, share and transfer knowledge and leverage the capabilities even with existing at different location, broaden different economy and among multiple people. The communication has been widely accepted in building the bridge among countries, regions and provides firms new opportunities, connects people and creates channels for development of business. Entrepreneurs in most of the developed and developing countries in West and America have been using wide range of ICT tools and techniques for product development, marketing, planning and other strategic purposes. ICT acts as an effective tool for the women entrepreneurs to develop and find opportunities in spite of various factors affecting adverse in some regions of the world. ICT enables women entrepreneurs to extend equal opportunities compared to male in growth and development of nation's economy and provides women with an avenue to express the development of their personalities and capabilities. ICT tools are acting as the major shield to develop business and extend growth beyond the boundaries which seems impossible in past two decades back. In a nut shell the ICT has become an integral part of the business sphere across the globe.

The revolution in the use of ICT tool can bring the entrepreneur from their social shell to express the dexterity and boost the economic growth. The use of ICT increases women capacities to share and access information and knowledge besides helpful and support to develop their entrepreneurial business activities and leads to promote women undertakings in broader space. ICT has enormous potential as a tool to enhance women's economic, political and social empowerment. Women entrepreneurs in particular can benefit from these to improve their access to information and network and to increase their competitiveness and market outreach of their businesses. In 2003, the Declaration of Principles of World Summit Information Society (WSIS) adopted by more than 175 countries emphasized the opportunities provided to the women through ICT development as follows:

- "We affirm that development of ICT provides enormous opportunities for women, who should be integral part of and key actors in the Information Society. We are committed to encouraging that the Information Society enables women empowerment and their full participation on the basis of equality in all spheres of society and in all decision-making processes. We should main stream a gender equality perspective using ICT as tool that end."
- Women entrepreneurs are playing an important role in the global quest for sustained economic development and social progress throughout the world. But in Indian context, though women have played a prominent role in the society, their entrepreneurial ability has not been properly tapped due lower status of women in the society. It is only from seventies, the role of women in process of the economic development has been explicitly recognised

by the Indian policy-makers. And thus, the development of women entrepreneurial has become an important aspect of plan priorities. A manifold of policies and programmes have been implemented for the development of women entrepreneurship in India.

- In spite of the various efforts taken by the Indian Government for the empowerment of women, particularly in economic and social spheres, still their participation remains low compared to male counterpart. The encouragement of women entrepreneurship in India seems difficult with various challenges at basic level but not impossible. It has been observed that women-led enterprises have shown a lower propensity to grow and higher propensity to exit under unfavorable industry and competitive conditions. Promoting women entrepreneurship in India should address the policy of producing a cadre of women leaders inclined towards taking risk and starting more and more business enterprises.
- Mostly female entrepreneurs in India are in the informal and micro sectors producing less sophisticated goods and services. Female owned firms are active in developing more domestic requirement product and also looking forward to market their products to other countries. But these entrepreneurs are less inclined to use ICT tools like e-mail and internet in their information interactions and services. Also, female owned businesses are substantially less profitable and innovative than male owned businesses due to low level access to market which will directly affect the investment and outward growth.
- Using information and communication technologies has not rooted in the daily activities of Indian women as compared to women in American and European regions. During the fast few years, India is encouraging ICT development and private sector development to sustain the growth in economy in wake of growth in population and unemployment. Entrepreneurial growth in respect to of women entrepreneurs has been regarded and is

given due consideration for growth in industrialization. Female entrepreneurs can play a significant role in fostering the development of the small business sector and facilitating the evolution of enterprise.

Women entrepreneurs especially in informal and micro sectors have grown in large number across the globe over the last decade and increasingly the entrepreneurial potentials of women have changed the rural economies in many parts of the world. Besides the star cases like Grameena Telephone Ladies in Bagladesh spearheaded by Nobel Laureate Muhammad Yunus there are many other successful women businesses using ICT in different parts of world in recent years. Richard Duncombe *et al.,* shows ELIF Business Solutions in Zambia, Busyincubator in Ghana as illustrative cases. The following are some of the illustrative cases of successful women enterprises using ICT in informal and micro sectors in India.

TECHNOWORLD

This data entry micro-enterprise was set up as a part of the Kudumbashree initiative. Members of various self-help groups with basic skills were selected to form the first ever women's group enterprise in data entry in Kerala State. The group was given a series of training programmes in data entry, software integration, marketing and accounting. The initiative had a budget of US$ 6445 raised through a bank loan, members' contributions and a small subsidy. The first client was Employee Provident Fund Department for the digitization of personnel records. The enterprise repaid all its initial loans within three years of commencing its operations. There are ten qualified members in the group both general and IT personnel. They are now employing a large number of other women for data entry work on a piece-rate basis.

Divine Computers

The local government advertised the State's IT@ School Programme in the local newspaper, calling for qualified applicants from below poverty-line families to start a group enterprise. A team of six determined women formed and mobilized a group loan of US$ 4,444 from the State Bank of Travancore under a Central Government Poverty Alleviation Scheme. The group members contributed US$ 222 while the rest of the funds was adjusted through a subsidy. The micro-enterprise is involved in the training of school students under the IT@ School Programme. The school collects monthly fees from the students and pays the loan installment and the rest is given to the women in Divine Group. The group consists of six members who are having computer training in areas such as desktop publishing and MS Office. Even one has passed a Computer Teacher Training Course.

Market for E-business and E-commerce

The project E-seva (E-services) was initiated as a tool to introduce ICT in the rural areas, especially to women in the district of West Godavari. Using ICT, the project provides the local people with access to various C2C (Citizen-to-Citizen) and C2G (Citizen-to-Government) services. Web-enabled rural kiosks termed E-seva centres, have been established at the mandal level. A unique feature about these centres is that they are run and managed by the women from self-help groups, positioning them as information leaders, and helping to bridge the gender divide. The ICT has played a critical role in turning the women groups as change agents while drawing strength from the project. This project replaces the traditional form of governance and its accompanying deficiencies with a modern, more open, transparent and responsive service delivery system.

These E-seva centres run on a district portal that allows access to various citizen centric services. These services range from the issuance of various certificates to getting information about programmes and also go to the extent of allowing citizens to network with each other for mutually beneficial transactions. Citizens can file grievances at these centres. Every grievance is acknowledged and transferred online for field action. They can also publicize their projects and goods through the portal for online auctions. Through the portal, the centres expect to provide a virtual meeting place for the citizens to discuss issues relating to their districts/villages, their problems and prospective solutions (http://www.westgodavari.org).

WOMEN ENTREPRENEURS – CHALLENGES

In developed countries, there is a phenomenal increase in number of women entrepreneurs after the World War II. In USA, women own 25 per cent of all business enterprises. In Canada, women own one-third of small business enterprises. In France, their percentage is one-fifth. In India, their percentage is 5.2 only in the year 1981. But as per the census of 2001, this figure has risen to 11.2 per cent. The low rate of women entrepreneurs compared to other parts of the world is mainly due to the various challenges faced by women entrepreneurs. Asian Development Bank (ADB) Report recognises women as "....a significant entrepreneurial force, contributing to local, national and regional economies and to poverty reduction, but they face different constraints and opportunities from those experienced by men."

In India, women are generally engaged in household activities which consume most of their time. As women are fully engaged in family nourishment, the women engaged in entrepreneurial activities have challenging demands for time. The greatest deterrent factor to women entrepreneurs is that they are women. Because of the patriarchal – male dominant – social order prevailing in India, women are deprived of involving themselves in the family business as well. Generally, women have no exposure to develop business plan, arranging finance, look for better resources, information on credit. As stated in a World Bank report " Socio-cultural norms and negative attitudes towards working women further discourage the women entrepreneurship even further."

Lack of women empowerment in the men dominated society creates foremost effect on the developing women at the society level. According to The Economist, "Lack of knowledge and the continuing treatment of women as second-class citizens keep them in a pervasive cycle of poverty." The mind set will directly affect the participation of women in business network and creating of positive outlook.

Low level of participation in the education and training had a direct impact on the women interested in undertaking entrepreneurial activity. Though government had taken firm steps to bring girls into regular education programme through strong initiatives and reforming the policies, women entrepreneurial development has not transpired in India. Much more effort is needed to bring these programmes and policies to the grass root level. Lack of basic school education system to females in the remote regions of India has created non-conducive milieu for promoting women entrepreneurs at later stages. As stated in the UNIDO report "Due to a lack of technical skills, confidence, strong individual involvement and the willingness to take risks, women are often unable to establish and sustain successful businesses."

The informal discrimination of looking down women as unsuccessful in business creates negative effect on investors in providing financial support to women started business enterprises. Undoubtedly, this will hinder women growth and development as entrepreneurs in terms of raising finance, taking credits, and developing long-term relations with other business partners. As observed in a report of UNIDO, "Lack of availability of finance to women started projects is the foremost reason for loosing charm in attracting customers, suppliers and distributors. Just the same way as women still face more barriers inside and outside the labour market despite education gains, women face additional barriers in the business environment despite their capabilities and business acumen."

The financial institutions are skeptical about the entrepreneurial abilities of women. The banker considers that granting loans to women entrepreneurs is more risky than that of men entrepreneurs. The banker stipulates unrealistic and unreasonable securities to grant loans to women entrepreneurs. According to a report by the United Nations Industrial Development Organization, "despite evidence that women's loan repayment rates are higher than men's, women still face more difficulties in obtaining credit, often due to discriminatory attitudes of banks and informal lending groups".

Knowledge of latest technological changes, technical know how, and education level of a person are main factors that affect entrepreneurial development. The literacy rate among women in India is at a very low level. Many women in developing nations lack the education needed to spur successful entrepreneurship. "Although great advances are being made in technology, many a woman's illiteracy structural difficulties and lack of access to technical training prevent the technology from being beneficial or even available to females."

Lack of female role models as women entrepreneurs deeply demotivates the individual to undertake the entrepreneurial activities. Entrepreneurial attributes urge to be successful in the business and become a role model for others. Due to the conventional pattern of business, networking and influence from the male dominated society very few women entrepreneurs have been named as role models in India and it happens only within these recent years.

SUCCESSFUL WOMEN ENTREPRENEURS OF INDIA

Government of India has taken many initiatives for empowerment of women and development of women entrepreneurs from the Fifth Five-year Plan (1974-78) onwards. Using ICT, many women have established themselves as successful entrepreneurs in India. The following is list of the most noted women entrepreneurs of India:

- Dr. Kiran Mazumdar-Shaw ,Chairperson and Managing Director of Biocon Ltd., started her business in 1978 with an initial investment of mere Rs. 10000. Her applications for loans were turned down by banks on three counts-biotechnology was a new word, the company lacked tangible assets and women entrepreneurs were still a rarity. Today, she is the richest women in India having assets more than Rs. 2100 crores and her company is the biggest bio-pharmaceutical firm in the country.

- Seven women formed Lizzat Papad Food Industry on the co-operative basis. At present it has become a trusted brand in food industries and employing over 50000 women.
- Veena Mathur, Chairperson of RBMI Bareilly, has started a school a two decade ago with just 5 students. Now, the school has turn around into a leading Management, Engineering, B.Pharm College with over 3000 students.
- Inira Krishna Murty Nooyi, Chairperson and Executive Officer of Pepsi Co., has shown her skill in Pepsi strategically in marketing of beverages and fast food business by merging Quaker and Tropicana into Pepsi.
- Shahnaz Hussain is the mother of all herbal cosmetics in world. Her supply chain consists of over 5000 products. Across globe, she has 650 salons in 104 countries. Her products have acquired distinctive global brand loyalty.
- Neelam Dhawan, Managing Director of Microsoft India, leads Microsoft sales and marketing operations in the country. After passing from Delhi's Faculty of Management Studies in 1982, she was keen on joining FMCG majors like Hidustan Lever and Asian Paints. But both the companies rejected Dhawan as they did not want women for marketing.
- Naina Lal Kidwai was the first Indian woman to graduate from Harvard Business School. According to the Economic Times, she is the first woman to head operations of a foreign bank - HSBC - in India.
- Sulajja Firodia Motwani, Joint Managing Director of Kinetic Engineering Ltd., is in-charge of company's overall business development activities. She was ranked among top 25 business entrepreneurs of the country and was chosen as the Global Leader of Tomorrow by the World Economic Forum.

- Ekta Kapoor, Creative Head of Balaji Telefilms, has dominated Indian television by producing more than eight television soaps. At the 6th Indian Telly Awards 2006, she bagged the Hall of Fame award for her contributions.

SUGGESTIONS FOR THE DEVELOPMENT OF WOMEN ENTREPRENEURS

- Right efforts and measures from all directions are required for the development of women entrepreneurs and their greater participation in the growth and development of Indian economy. The following efforts and measures should be initiated by the Government as well as non-governmental organizations for the effective development of women entrepreneurship.
- Long-term strategies for addressing the cultural and social barriers, which are detrimental to women entrepreneurship, should be undertaken forthwith. For this the government should take appropriate measures to provide educational to all girls which enhances women potentialities and promotes women entrepreneurship in later periods of their life. Programmes for encouraging entrepreneurship should be incorporated from secondary education and Intermediate education levels which paves the way for girls to be aware of business opportunities which acts as catalyst for women entrepreneurship and eventually women empowerment. Technical skills should be taught in Polytechnics and Industrial Training Institutes by giving emphasis on training-cum-production workshops.
- Efforts should be taken to promote ICT field as not only as male domain and encourage women to take up leadership role in technology intensive businesses. Certainly, this strategy will enable women to take advantage of entrepreneurial opportunities provided by ICT.
- The semi-literate women besides getting trained in business technology and financial management are also

need to be educated about the importance of marketing their produce. Government incentives and assistance is the need of the hour for marketing the products produced by women enterprises. In Industrial Exhibitions provision should be made for the display and sale of the products made by women also.

- To mitigate the need for capital in the absence of tangible assets and securities offered by the women entrepreneurs, micro-finance, which is the best alternative to financing funds from formal methods for meeting day-to-day expenses, should be encouraged. In the words of Morduch, "Micro-finance appears, therefore, to offer a win-win solution where financial institutions and poor clients benefit." These institutions have also proven the ability to reach poor individuals, particularly women that have been difficult to reach through alternative approaches.
- Access to capital in the prime concern of any women entrepreneur but capital itself is not enough to make an enterprise into a successful enterprise. Apart from providing finance, banks and other financial institutions have to undertake programmes of assisting the women entrepreneur to support networks, technical training before granting loans to women as well as after granting the loans.
- Women Guidance Cells should be set up to address the various problems of women entrepreneurs throughout the state. These cells provide a platform for women entrepreneurs, who are already in business and have a vivid insight into the challenges and suggestive actions needed to improve women entrepreneurship, to voice their problems to Governmental agencies for policy actions.
- Access to capital, technology and technical assistance were all found more problematic for women entrepreneurs outside the metropolitan cities. Efforts should be taken to bridge the access gap between large cities and small towns and rural areas.

CONCLUSION

Independence brought promise of equality of opportunity in all spheres to the Indian women and laws guaranteeing for their equal right of participation in political process and equal opportunities and right in education and employment were enacted. It is estimated that women entrepreneurs may be more than 20 per cent of total entrepreneurs in another decade. The challenges and opportunities provided to the women of Information Society are turning them fast from job seekers to job creators. But unfortunately, the government sponsored development activities have benefited only a small section of women. The large majority of them are still unaffected by change and development. Government of India should draw up plan for empowering women entrepreneurs through training and capacity building programmes and encouraging the use of ICT. The vision should be within the next decade Indian women entrepreneurs should be found in every field – be it biotechnology or information technology; be it rural or cosmopolitan city; be it small scale or medium scale or large scale entrepreneurship, women should enter every sector.

REFERENCES

Weber, Max, Proslertant Ethic and Spirit of Capitalism, New York: Scribner, 1904; English Translation 1930.

Shumpeter, Joseph, Capitalism, Socialism and Democracy, New York: Harper and Brothers, 1942.

Duncombe, Richard *et al.*, Supporting Women ICT Based Enterprises: A Hand Book for Agencies in Development, IDPM, University of Manchester.

Ibid.

Asian Development Bank, Country Gender Assessment: Kyrgyz Republi, Manila, 2005.

World Bank Report, Environment for Women's Entrepreneurship in the Middle East, Washington DC.

The Female Poverty Traps, the Economist, Dt:, May 8, 2001.

United Nations Industrial Development Organization, Developing Rural and Women Entrepreneurship, Vienna, 2003.

Ibid.

United Nations Industrial Development Organization (UNIDO.), "Women, Industry and Technology," Women in Industry Series, Vienna. 1995

Women Entrepreneurs in Poorest Countries face Formidable Challenges, Including Lack of Training, Credit, say Speakers at Brussels Forum, Presss Release, May 21, 2001.

Morduch J., "The Microfinance Promise", *Journal of Economic Literature*, XXXVII, December.

15

Women Entrepreneurship Catalyst for Women Empowerment

G. Nazneen Begum*

Women owned businesses are highly increasing in the economies of almost all countries. The hidden entrepreneurial potentials of women have gradually been changing with the growing sensitivity to the role and economic status in the society. Skill, knowledge and adaptability in business are the main reasons for women to emerge into business ventures. 'Women Entrepreneur' is a person who accepts challenging role to meet her personal needs and become economically independent. A strong desire to do something positive is an inbuilt quality of entrepreneurial women, who is capable of contributing values in both family and social life. With the advent of media, women are aware of their own traits, rights and also the work situations. The glass ceilings are shattered and women are found indulged in every line of business from pappad to power cables. The challenges and opportunities provided to the women of digital era are growing rapidly that the job seekers are turning into job creators. They are flourishing as designers, interior decorators, exporters, publishers, garment manufacturers and still exploring new avenues of economic participation. The additional business

* M.Com., M.Phil., M.B.A., Research Scholar, S.V., University, Tirupathi, A.P.

opportunities that are recently approaching for women entrepreneurs are:

- Eco-friendly technology.
- Bio-technology.
- IT enabled enterprises.
- Event management.
- Tourism industry.
- Tele-communication.
- Plastic materials.
- Vermiculture.
- Mineral water.
- Sericulture.
- Floriculture.
- Herbal and health care.
- Food, fruits and vegetable processing.

Empowering women entrepreneurs is essential for achieving the goals of sustainable development and the bottlenecks hindering their growth must be eradicated to entitle full participation in the business.

Apart from training programmes, newsletters, mentoring, trade fairs and exhibitions also can be a source for entrepreneurial development. As a result, the desired outcomes of the business are quickly achieved and more of remunerative business opportunities are found. Henceforth, promoting entrepreneurship among women is certainly a short-cut to rapid economic growth and development. Let us try to eliminate all forms of gender discrimination and thus allow women to be an entrepreneur at par with men. The Indian sociological set up has been traditionally a male dominate done. Women are considered as weaker sex and always to depend on men folk in their family and outside, throughout their life. They are left with lesser commitments and kept as a dormant force for a quite long time. The Indian culture made them only sub ordinates and executors of the decisions made by other male members, in the basic family structure. The traditional set up is changing in the modern era. The transformation of social fabric of the Indian society, in terms of increased educational status of women and varied aspirations for better living, necessitated a change in the life style of Indian women.

Indian families do have the privilege of being envied by the westerners, since women here are taking more responsibilities in bringing up children and maintaining a better home with love and affection. At the family level, the task of coordinating various activities in a much effective manner, without feeling the pinch of inconveniences, is being carried out by the women folk. Thus, the Indian women have basic characters in themselves in the present sociological and cultural setup as follows:

- Indian women are considered as Sakthi, which means source of power.
- Effectively coordinating the available factors and resources.
- Efficient execution of decisions imposed on them.
- Clear vision and ambition on the improvement of family and children.
- Patience and bearing the sufferings on behalf of others.

But still the Indian women entrepreneurs are facing some major constraints like –

- *Lack of Confidence* – In general, women lack confidence in their strength and competence. To a certain extent, this situation is changing among Indian women and yet to face a tremendous change to increase the rate of growth in entrepreneurship.
- *Socio-cultural Barriers* – Women's family and personal obligations are sometimes a great barrier for succeeding in business career. Only few women are able to manage both home and business efficiently, devoting enough time to perform all their responsibilities in priority.
- *Market-oriented Risks* – Stiff competition in the market and lack of mobility of women make the dependence of women entrepreneurs on middleman indispensable.

Many business women find it difficult to capture the market and make their products popular.

- *Motivational Factors* – Self-motivation can be realized through a mind set for a successful business, attitude to take up risk. Other factors are family support, Government policies, financial assistance and also the environment suitable for women to establish business units.
- *Knowledge in Business Administration* – Women must be educated and trained constantly to acquire the skills and knowledge in all the functional areas of business management.
- *Awareness about the Financial Assistance* – Various institutions in the financial sector extend their maximum support in the form of incentives, loans, schemes etc. Even then every woman entrepreneur may not be aware of all the assistance provided by the institutions.
- *Exposed to the Training Programmes* – Training programmes and workshops are available through the social and welfare associations. Such programmes are really useful to new, rural and young entrepreneurs who want to set up a small and medium scale unit on their own.
- *Identifying the Available Resources* – Women are hesitant to find out the access to cater their needs in the financial and marketing areas. They are not enterprising and dynamic to optimize the resources in the form of reserves, assets mankind or business volunteers.

Women Entrepreneurs may be defined as the women or a group of women who initiate, organize and operate a business enterprise. Government of India has defined women entrepreneurs as an enterprise owned and controlled by a women having a minimum financial interest of 51 per cent of the capital and giving at least 51 per cent of employment generated in the enterprise to women. Like a male entrepreneurs a women entrepreneur has many functions. They should explore the prospects of starting new enterprise;

undertake risks, introduction of new innovations, coordination administration and control of business and providing effective leadership in all aspects of business.

PROBLEMS OF WOMEN ENTREPRENEURS IN INDIA

- The greatest deterrent to women entrepreneurs is that they are women. A kind of patriarchal – male dominant social order is the building block to them in their way towards business success. Male members think it a big risk financing the ventures run by women.
- The financial institutions are skeptical about the entrepreneurial abilities of women. The bankers consider women loonies as higher risk than men loonies.
- Entrepreneurs usually require finançial assistance of some kind to launch their ventures - be it a formal bank loan or money from a savings account. The women entrepreneurs lack access to external funds due to their inability to provide tangible security. Very few women have the tangible property in hand.
- Women's family obligations also bar them from becoming successful entrepreneurs in both developed and developing nations.
- Indian women give more emphasis to family ties and relationships. Married women have to make a fine balance between business and home.
- Another argument is that women entrepreneurs have low-level management skills. They have to depend on office staffs and intermediaries, to get things done, especially, the marketing and sales side of business.
- The male - female competition is another factor, which develop hurdles to women entrepreneurs in the business management process. The confidence to travel across day and night and even different regions and states are less found in women compared to male entrepreneurs. This shows the low level freedom of expression and freedom of mobility of the women entrepreneurs.

- Knowledge of alternative source of raw materials availability and high negotiation skills are the basic requirement to run a business, which affect women entrepreneur's business adventures.
- Knowledge of latest technological changes, know how, and education level of the person are significant factor that affect business.
- Low-level risk taking attitude is another factor affecting women folk decision to get into business. Low-level education provides low-level self-confidence and self-reliance to the women folk to engage in business.
- Achievement motivation of the women folk found less compared to male members. The low level of education and confidence leads to low level achievement and advancement motivation among women folk.
- Finally high production cost of some business operations adversely affects the development of women entrepreneurs.

Women are generally perceived as home makers with little to do with economy or commerce. But this picture is changing. In Modern India, more and more women are taking up entrepreneurial activity especially in medium and small-scale enterprises. Even as women are receiving education, they face the prospect of unemployment. In this background, self-employment is regarded as a cure to generate income. The Planning commission as well as the Indian government recognises the need for women to be part of the mainstream of economic development. Women entrepreneurship is seen as an effective strategy to solve the problems of rural and urban poverty.

Traditionally, women in India have been generally found in low productive sectors such as agriculture and household activities. Human Development Report 2004 ranks India 103 in Gender related Development Index (GDI). As per 2001 census; women constitute nearly half of India's population. Out of this total, 72 per cent were engaged in agriculture, 21.7 per cent in other non agricultural pursuits with only 6.3 per cent in household industries.

Women entrepreneurs in India are handicapped in the matter of organizing and running businesses on account of their generally low levels of skills and for want of support system. The transition from home-maker to sophisticated business woman is not that easy. But the trend is changing. Women across India are showing an interest to be economically independent. Women are coming forth to the business arena with ideas to start small and medium enterprises. They are willing to be inspired by role models – the experience of other women in the business arena.

The role of women entrepreneurs is especially relevant in the situation of large scale unemployment that the country faces. The modern large scale industry cannot absorb much of labour as it is capital intensive. The small-scale industry plays an important role absorbing around 80 per cent of the employment. The myth that women cannot engage in productive employment needs to be dispelled. They can be encouraged to set up small and medium scale industries on their own initiative. Entrepreneurship development for women is an important factor in economic development of India. Rural women can be encouraged to start cottage industries. Rural based micro-enterprises have been encouraged by the government by various schemes-such as Integrated Rural Development Programme (IRDP), Training of Rural Youth for Self-employment (TRYSEM), and Development of Women and Children in Rural Areas (DWCRA). The aim is to remove poverty through entrepreneurial programmes.

When making the decision to become an entrepreneur, the first question that often comes to mind is: '*What business should I start*?'. Here are some of the suitable and practical ideas for home-based women entrepreneurs and work at home moms.

- Virtual Assistant.
- Blogging.
- Home Staging Business.
- Handcrafted Items.

- Herb Farming.
- Personal Chef.
- Elderly Care Business.
- Consulting.
- Medical Claims Billing.

HOW TO DEVELOP WOMEN ENTREPRENEURS?

- Consider women as specific target group for all developmental programmes.
- Better educational facilities and schemes should be extended to women folk from government part.
- Adequate training programme on management skills to be provided to women community.
- Encourage women's participation in decision-making.
- Vocational training to be extended to women community that enables them to understand the production process and production management.
- Training on professional competence and leadership skill to be extended to women entrepreneurs.
- Training and counseling on a large scale of existing women entrepreneurs to remove psychological causes like lack of self-confidence and fear of success.
- Activities in which women are trained should focus on their marketability and profitability.
- To encourage more passive women entrepreneurs the Women training programme should be organized that taught to recognise her own psychological needs and express them.
- State finance corporations and financing institutions should permit by statute to extend purely trade related finance to women entrepreneurs.
- Women's development corporations have to gain access to open-ended financing.
- The financial institutions should provide more working capital assistance both for small-scale venture and large scale ventures.

- Making provision of micro-credit system and enterprise credit system to the women entrepreneurs at local level.
- Repeated gender sensitisation programmes should be held to train financiers to treat women with dignity and respect as persons in their own right.
- Infrastructure, in the form of industrial plots and sheds, to set up industries is to be provided by state run agencies.
- A Women Entrepreneur's Guidance Cell set up to handle the various problems of women entrepreneurs all over the state.
- District Industries Centres and Single Window Agencies should make use of assisting women in their trade and business guidance.
- Programmes for encouraging entrepreneurship among women are to be extended at local level.
- More governmental schemes to motivate women entrepreneurs to engage in small-scale and large-scale business ventures.
- Continuous monitoring and improvement of training programmes.

Most successful women entrepreneur posses the following traits:

- *She is Ambitious* – A successful woman entrepreneur is extremely ambitious, has an inner urge or drive to transform an idea into reality. Every successful woman entrepreneur is truly determined to achieve goals and make her business flourish. In-depth knowledge of the field is essential to success. She comes with new innovative solutions to old problems to tide over issues.
- *She is Confident* – A successful woman entrepreneur is confident in her ability. She is ready to learn from others, seek help from experts if it means adding value to her goals. She is optimistic and is more willing to take risks.

- *She is Open and Willing to Learn* – A successful woman entrepreneur keeps abreast of changes, as she is fully aware of the importance of evolving changes. She is ahead of her competitors and thrives on changes. She adapts her business to changes in technology or service expectations of her clients.
- *She is Cost Conscious* – A successful woman entrepreneur prepares realistic budget estimates. She provides cost-effective quality services to her clients. With minimized cost of operations, she is able to drive her team to maximize profits and reap its benefits.
- *She Values Teamwork and Loyalty* – She has the ability to work with all levels of people. She is keen on maintaining relationships and communicates clearly and effectively. This helps her to negotiate even sensitive issues easily. She is empathetic to people around her and possess good networking skills that help her to expand contacts and make use of opportunities.
- *She can Balance Home and Work* – She is cautious of not becoming a workaholic, a successful woman entrepreneur is good at balancing diverse aspects of life.
- *She is Conscious of her Responsibility to Society* – A successful woman entrepreneur is willing to share her success with the society. She is committed to help others and enjoys doing it.

Despite all the social hurdles, many women have become successful in their works. A list of some of the powerful women in various fields such as, politics, business are listed below:

List of Some Successful Women

1. Sonia Gandhi, President, Congress Party,
2. Indra Nooyi, Chief Executive—designate, Pepsi Co.,
3. Lalita Gupte and Kalpana Morparia, Joint Managing Directors, ICICI Bank,
4. Vidya Manohar Chhabria, Chairman, Jumbo Group,
5. Simone Tata, Managing Director (former) Lakme,

6. Indu Jain, Chairperson (former) The Times Group,
7. Neelam Dhawan, Managing Director, Microsoft India,
8. Akhila Srinivasan, Managing Director, Shriram Investments Ltd.,
9. Chanda Kocchar, Executive Director, ICICI Bank,
10. Ekta Kapoor, Creative Director, Balaji Telefilms,
11. Jyoit Naik, President, Lijjat Papad,
12. Kiran Mazumdar-Shaw, Chairman and Managing Director, Biocon,
13. Lalita D Gupte, Joint Managing Director, ICICI Bank,
14. Naina Lal Kidwai, Deputy CEO, HSBC,
15. Preetha Reddy, Managing Director, Apollo Hospitals,
16. Priya Paul, Chairman, Apeejay Park Hotels,
17. Ranjana Kumar, Chariman, NABARD,
18. Ravina Raj Kohil, Media personality and Ex-President, STAR News,
19. Renuka Ramnath, CEO, ICICI Ventures,
20. Ritu Kumar, Fashion Designer,
21. Ritu Nanda, CEO, Escolife,
22. Shahnaz Hussain, CEO, Shahnaz Herbals,
23. Sulajja Firodia Motwani, Joint MD, Kinetic Engineering,
24. Tarjani Vakil, former Chairman and Managing Director, EXIM Bank.

In India, although women constitute the majority of the total population, the entrepreneurial world is still a male dominated one. Highly educated, technically sound and professionally qualified women should be encouraged for managing their own business, rather than dependent on wage employment outlets. The unexplored talents of young women can be identified, trained and used for various types of industries to increase the productivity in the industrial sector. A desirable environment is necessary for every woman to inculcate entrepreneurial values and involve greatly in business dealings. The educated women do not want to limit their lives in the four walls of the house. They demand equal respect from their partners. However, Indian women have to go a long way to achieve equal rights and position because traditions are deep rooted in Indian society.

REFERENCES

Anna V. (1990), Socio-economic Basis of Women Entrepreneurship. *Sedme,* 17(1): 17-47.

Association of Women Entrepreneurs of Karnataka (AWAKE). 1993. Policy-Practice Gap With Reference to Collateral Security. Bangalore, India: AWAKE.

Bhasin, Kamla. (1994), What is Patriarchy? New Dehli: Raj Press.

Brush, Candida. (1992), "Research on Women Business Owners: Past Trends, A New Perspective and Future Directions," Entrepreneurship: Theory and Practice 16, No. 4: 5.30.

Chatterjee, Purvita. (2001), "India: Children Replace Husband as a Focal Point in Women's Life." Business Line (August 14): 1.

Chua, Peter, Kum-Kum Bhavani and John Foran. (2000), "Women, Culture and Development: A New Paradigm for Development Studies?. Ethnic and Racial Studies 23, No. 5: 820.42.

Das, Mallika. (1999), "Work-family Conflicts of Indian Women Entrepreneurs: A Preliminary Report," *New England Journal of Entrepreneurship* 2, No. 2: 39.47.

Deivasenapathy P. (1986), Entrepreneurial Success: Influence of Certain Personal Variables. *Indian Journal of Social Work,* 46(4): 547-555.

Pareek (1992), *Entrepreneurial Role Stress.* Mimeographed, Ahmedabad: Indian Institute of Management.

16

Problems and Prospects of Women Entrepreneurship
Streamlining through A Systematic Approach

G.V. Chandra Mouli*
G. Swetha**

ABSTRACT

The Indian economy has been witnessing a drastic change since mid - 1991, with new Policies of economic liberalization, globalization and privatization initiated by the Indian government. India has great entrepreneurial potential. At present, women involvement in economic activities is marked by a low work participation rate, excessive concentration in the unorganized sector. Women entrepreneurs have been making a significant impact in all segments of the economy in Canada, Britain, Germany, Australia, India and America. According to a report put out by the CIBC, by 2010 one million women will own a small business. Women owned businesses are highly increasing in the economies of almost all countries. The hidden entrepreneurial potentials of women have gradually been changing with the growing sensitivity to the role and economic status in the society. Skill, knowledge and adaptability in business are the main reasons for

* Incharge and Assistant Professor, Global College of Engineering and Technoogy, Kadapa, A.P.

** H.O.D., Sree Venkateswara College of Engineering, Tirupati, A.P.

women to emerge into business ventures'. Women Entrepreneur' is a person who accepts challenging role to meet her personal needs and become economically independent. In India, although women constitute the majority of the total population, the entrepreneurial world is still a male dominated one. Women in advanced nations are recognised and are more prominent in the business world. The challenges faced by women entrepreneurs are Financial Constraints, lack of access to technology, marketing problems, lack of schemes awareness, production problems, health problems, gender gap, Lack of Visibility as Strategic Leaders, Differential Information and Assistance Needs, Occupational closure and segregation, psychological factors, multiple roles, lack of education, knowledge and experience, physical infrastructure, Lack of family support, Capital, Confidence and Faith. Guidelines framed as a solution to these problems can help women entrepreneurs to deal with these problems effectively.

INTRODUCTION

Entrepreneurship is the core of economic development. It is a multi-dimensional task and essentially a creative activity. Entrepreneur is the key factor of entrepreneurship and now women have been recognised as successful entrepreneurs as they have qualities desirable and relevant for entrepreneurship development. Women Entrepreneurs may be defined as the women or a group of women who initiate, organize and operate a business enterprise. Government of India has defined Women Entrepreneurs as an enterprise owned and controlled by a women having a minimum financial interest of 51 per cent of the capital and giving at least 51 per cent of employment generated in the enterprise to women. In the process of entrepreneurship, women have to face various problems associated with entrepreneurship and these problems get doubled because of her dual role as a wage earner and a home-maker. There are several factors for emergence of women entrepreneurship in India such as family background, motivating and facilitating factors, ambitions, attitudes of family and society, government policy of funds, marketing systems, training programmes etc.

During the last two decades, Indian women have entered the field of entrepreneurship in greatly increasing numbers. With the emergence and growth of their businesses, they have contributed to the global economy and to their surrounding communities. These women entrepreneurs have entered many industries and sectors. The routes women have followed to take leadership roles in business are varied. Yet, most women business owners have overcome or worked to avoid obstacles and challenges in creating their businesses. The presence of women in the workplace driving small and entrepreneurial organizations creates a tremendous impact on employment and business environments.

Indian women business owners are changing the face of businesses of today, both literally and figuratively. The dynamic growth and expansion of women-owned businesses is one of the defining trends of the past decade, and all indications are that it will continue unabated. For more than a decade, the number of women-owned businesses have grown at one-and-a-half to two times the rate of all businesses. Even more important, the expansion in revenues and employment has far exceeded the growth in numbers. The result of these trends is that women-owned businesses span the entire range of business life cycle and business success, whether the measuring stick is revenue, employment or longevity. This strengthens the view that all governmental programmes and policies should target at strengthening women's entrepreneurship in their native lands.

Women entrepreneurs need to be lauded for their increased utilisation of modern technology, increased investments, finding a niche in the export market, creating a sizable employment for others and setting the trend for other women entrepreneurs in the organized sector. While women entrepreneurs have demonstrated their potential, the fact remains that they are capable of contributing much more than what they already are. In order to harness their potential and for their continued growth and development, it is necessary to formulate appropriate strategies for stimulating, supporting and sustaining their efforts in this direction. Such a strategy needs to be in congruence with field realities, and should especially take cognizance of the problems women entrepreneurs face within the current system.

PUSH-PULL FACTORS AND WOMEN IN BUSINESS

Women entrepreneurs engaged in business due to push and pull factors. Which encourage women to have an independent occupation and stands on their legs. A sense towards independent decision-making on their life and career is the motivational factor behind this urge. Saddled with household chores and domestic responsibilities women want to get independence. Under the influence of these factors the women entrepreneurs choose a profession as a challenge and as an urge to do some thing new. Such situation is described as pull factors. While in push factors women engaged in business activities due to family compulsion and the responsibility is thrust upon them.

CHALLENGES FACED BY WOMEN ENTREPRENEURS

1. *Financial Problems:* Finance is a most important aspect of any business. Non-availability of long-term finance, regular and frequent need of working capital and long procedure to avail financial help was found to be the financial problems faced by respondents based on the multiple responses given by them.
2. *Marketing Problems:* During the process of marketing of products women entrepreneurs faced certain problems *viz.,* poor location of shop, lack of transport facility and tough competition from larger and established units. Difficulty in affording own vehicle was a major factor causing marketing problem.
3. *Production Problems:* Production problems faced by maximum respondents were non-availability of raw-material. This is one of the reasons for the slow growth

of women entrepreneurs. Other production problems were non-availability of machine or equipment, lack of training facility and non-availability of labour. Major causable factors leading to production problems were high cost of required machine or equipment.

4. *Health Problems:* Major health problems faced by women entrepreneurs were tension, backache, eyestrain fatigue and headache women respondents faced the problem of feeling fatigued after returning home. Causable factors were lack of rest and sleep and heavy schedule.
5. *Work Place Problems:* The work place facility problems faced were *viz.*, inadequate work place for water, less entrance for natural light and improper space for work. Causable factors were water shortage, less entrance for natural light and lack of sufficient area for business. Major problems faced by women entrepreneurs were poor location of unit, tough competition from larger and established units because in all the enterprises work was done manually so it was very tough to compete with those enterprises in which electrical equipments and big machineries were used.
6. *Other Problems:* Other problems were lack of transport facility, lack of time for household work, non-availability of raw material, heavy schedule and lack of time for rest and sleep leading to mental tension and fatigue. The factors causable to these problems were difficulty in affording own vehicle, product not being popular, heavy schedule of work and long job hours.
7. *Lack of Visibility as Strategic Leaders*: Changing the perceptions about the likely success of women-owned businesses depends on increasing women's visibility in leadership positions within the greater business community. In an assessment of women's presence as CEOs or Directors of large business enterprises, it has been anticipated that the exodus of women to entrepreneurial growth firms might be because women

believe that have greater representation in strategic leadership positions in privately-held or family-owned firms as they provide better opportunities for leadership than available to women in publicly-traded companies.

8. *Differential Information and Assistance Needs*: Another significant need of many women business owners is obtaining the appropriate assistance and information needed to take the business to the next level of growth. Those who were just starting their ventures, requested assistance and training in implementing the business idea, identifying initial sources of financing, and advertising/promotion. The entrepreneurs, who were already established, had a somewhat different set of needs including financing for expansion and increasing sales.
9. *Family Influences on Women Entrepreneurs*: The overlapping of the family and the firm is not significant for women business owners. As the boundaries between the firm and the family tend to be indistinct, women operating family businesses face a unique set of issues related to personal identity, role conflict, loyalties, family relationships, and attitudes towards authority. Additionally, family businesses owned by women are at a disadvantage financially and are forced to rely on internal resources of funding rather than outside sources. The critical role of family in business also emerges in cross-cultural studies which show a women relying heavily on the family for start-up capital.
10. *Another study had identified ten most desired needs of fast growth entrepreneurs:*
    - *(i)* Using cash flow to make operational decisions.
    - *(ii)* Financing growth.
    - *(iii)* Increasing the value of the business.
    - *(iv)* Compensation for self and associates.
    - *(v)* Hiring, training and motivating for growth.
    - *(vi)* Succeeding in a rapidly changing world.

(*vii*) Successful selling.

(*viii*) Sales force management.

(*ix*) Management success.

(*x*) Problems and pitfalls of growth.

IMPORTANT PROBLEMS FACED BY WOMEN ENTREPRENEURS IN INDIA

1. Women hardly interact with other women who are successful entrepreneurs. This results in a negative impact on their networking skills.
2. The areas, where one can see women acting as entrepreneurs, is in the very typical women's sectors. This is also the area, where women are accepted in society to be experts in and thus have the capacity for entrepreneurial activities.
3. It is clear, that women have the responsibility of getting children and taking care of them. Very few societies accept fathers taking over the role of staying home and taking care of the children. Once these children are old enough to take care for themselves, they have to bear an additional responsibility of taking care of elder parents. If they want to become entrepreneurs, the society expects them to be able to do both: take care of family and home and do business.
4. Women are very critical when it comes to themselves – can I really do this, am I good enough, may be I have to learn more, others can do it better. It is quite interesting that many successful women have been educated in only girls colleges and schools, which often deliver a safe environment to try out ones personal strengths, learn to overcome weaknesses and be proud of oneself.
5. Discrimination – it is hard to believe but women are still treated differently in our society. Women do get lower salaries compared to men doing the same job, women do not have access to men dominated networks who take their decisions about successors in the company during golf plays or sauna meetings.

6. Missing networks – through centuries business men have build up their networks but women still have to learn to catch up.
7. A lot of women tell stories about not being taken serious by bankers, when they wanted to get a loan for their business. Often enough, they have to bring their husbands or fathers to be able to be heard and receive financing. So, the domination of men in the banking world is a problem.

HOW TO DEVELOP WOMEN ENTREPRENEURS?

- Consider women as specific target group for all developmental programmes.
- Better educational facilities and schemes should be extended to women folk from government part.
- Adequate training programme on management skills to be provided to women community.
- Training on professional competence and leadership skill to be extended to women entrepreneurs.
- Continuous monitoring and improvement of training programmes.
- A Women Entrepreneur's Guidance Cell set up to handle the various problems of women entrepreneurs all over the state.

STEPS NEED TO BE INITIATED FOR WOMEN ENTREPRENEURIAL DEVELOPMENT IN INDIA

A possible set of three inter-linked and inter-dependent clusters of recommendations can be aimed at 'pushing' a larger number of women entrepreneurs towards growth opportunities, unlocking their potential as creators of wealth and jobs, and providing a more conducive legal and regulatory framework. These recommendations can also ensure the proper positioning of 'pull mechanisms' to enable the growth-oriented women entrepreneurs to expand and grow in terms of investments, markets and profits.

1. *Prioritizing and Pushing at the Micro-level:* There is a large and seemingly ever-increasing number of women

entrepreneurs operating in micro-enterprises and in the informal economy. They can be facilitated to grow into sustainable, formally registered and large enterprises with the help of following actions:–

- Conducting gender analysis for all entrepreneurial support programmes.
- Gathering data on women and men entrepreneurs.
- Applying 'target group segmentation' to women entrepreneurs.
- Using targeted approaches for priority categories in order to provide additional 'push' to women entrepreneurs to the next level of growth.
- Promoting mobilization and organization of representative associations.
- Examining differential impacts of governmental policies, programmes and actions.
- Promoting development of demand-led supports for women entrepreneurs.
- Promoting more flexible and innovative financial products by banks.

2. *Unlocking and Unfettering Institutional Framework:* Policies, laws and overall regulatory environment are frequently seen as barriers and disincentives to expansion and growth. However, they need to be promoted in such a way that women entrepreneurs see the advantages of and benefits that come with compliance.
   - Reviewing impact of existing and new instruments on women entrepreneurs.
   - Identifying those instruments that act as barriers to expansion and growth.
   - Modifying or dismantling these instruments.
   - Taking account of the social and cultural contexts affecting policy implementation and redress inequalities and abnormalities.

- Making use of IT and associations so as to minimize the administrative burdens on women entrepreneurs.
- Holding regular consultations with key factors like women entrepreneurs, women entrepreneurs' associations, financial institutions, etc., to review progress and identify new bottlenecks.

3. *Projecting and Pulling to Grow and Support the Winners:* The first two sets of recommendations are aimed at trying to 'push' more women entrepreneurs into growth situations as well as ensuring that laws and regulations do not stand in their way. The third possible recommendation relates to facilitating and 'pulling' the women entrepreneurs into situations where they can actively pursue growth strategies.
   - Providing incentives for expansion and growth after removing barriers and disincentives.
   - Encouraging and rewarding dynamic representative associations of women entrepreneurs.
   - Promoting strong links and synergies with existing major economic players.
   - Profiling the economic and social contributors among women entrepreneurs to the national economy.
   - Promoting and rewarding programmes that serve women entrepreneurs.
   - Making full use of data gathered to inform new policies, programmes and supportive actions.
   - Ensuring synergies between *(a)* women related ministry *(b)* economic ministry *(c)* welfare and social development ministry in the government.

GUIDELINES FOR A SUCCESSFUL WOMEN ENTREPRENEUR

Following guidelines have been recommended for becoming a successful women entrepreneur:

1. Entrepreneur should keep abreast of knowledge about new techniques, financial institutions, training institutions and marketing linkages. Some agencies working for women entrepreneurs are:

(a) SISI (Small Industry Service Institute).

(b) DIC (District Industry Centre).

(c) STEP (Science and Technology Entrepreneurship Park).

(d) Behavioural Science Centres.

(e) Indian Institute of Technology (Delhi).

2. *Prior to selection of area for development enterprise information about following aspects must be collected:*

   (a) Site or location.

   (b) Physical facilities.

   (c) Transportation facilities.

   (d) Place for disposal of waste material.

3. Self-help mutually aided groups must be formulated for overcoming common entrepreneurial problems.

4. Women should shift to the non-traditional sectors of entrepreneurship in order to earn more.

STRATEGIES FOR WOMEN ENTREPRENEURS TO SUCCEED

- Create a Strong Network.
- Consider Certifying as a Women-owned Business.
- Understand the Power of the Internet.
- Learn New Ways to Balance Work and Life.
- Get Inspiration and Advice From by Other Women Succeeding in Business.
- Women's Business News.

CONCLUSION

Women entrepreneurs faced constraints in aspects of financial, marketing production, work place facility and health problems. Financial problems faced were non-availability of long-term finance, regular and frequent need of working capital. Poor location of shop and lack of transport facility were major marketing problems. Production problems included the problem of non-availability of raw material. Women entrepreneurs also faced problem of improper water and space facility. Guidelines framed as a solution to these problems can help women entrepreneurs to deal with these problems effectively. With relevant education, work experience, improving economic conditions and financial opportunities, more women around the world are creating and sustaining successful business ventures. This will not only have an impact on the economies of the countries in which women own their businesses but also will change the status of women in those societies. It is likely that, as we begin this millennium, this will be the century of the entrepreneur in general and of the women entrepreneur in particular.

REFERENCES

Ahlawat, T. (1999), Impact of Financial Assistance Schemes on Economic Empowerment of Women.

Amulun, N. and A. Kumar. (1992), "Entrepreneurship Development in Orissa: Some Issues."

Kapoor, K. (1998), Entrepreneurial Behaviour: A Study of Selected Women Entrepreneurs.

Reddi, P.N. (1991), "Problems of Women Entrepreneurs.

Alvarez, S.A., and Meyer, G.D. (1998), Why do Women Become Entrepreneurs? *Frontiers of Entrepreneurship Research*, Wellesley, MA: Babson College.

Anna, A.L., Chandler, G. N., Jansen, E., and Mero, N. P. (2000), Women Business Owners in Traditional and Non-traditional Industries," *Journal of Business Venturing.*

Ben-Yoseph, M., Gundry, L.K., and Maslyk-Musial, E. (1994), Women Entrepreneurs in the United States and Poland, *Kobieta I Biznes.*

Ben-Yoseph, M., and Gundry, L.K. (1997), Teaching about Women Managers and Women Entrepreneurs Across Cultures, *Journal of Developmental Entrepreneurship.*

Birley, Sue (1989), Female Entrepreneurs; Are they Really Different? *Journal of Small Business Management*, Summer.

Brush, C. (1992), Research on Women Business Owners: Past Trends, A New Perspective and Future Directions, *Entrepreneurship: Theory and Practice.*

Brush, C. (1997), Women-Owned Businesses: Obstacles and Opportunities, *Journal of Developmental Entrepreneurship.*

Brush, C., and Hisrich, R. (1988), Women Entrepreneurs: Strategic Origins Impact on Growth. *Frontiers of Entrepreneurship Research.* Wellesley, MA: Babson College.

Clark, T., and James, F. (1992), Women-owned Businesses: Dimensions and Policy Issues. *Economic Development Quarterly.*

Gundry, L.K., and Welsch, H.P. (1994), Differences in Familial Influence among Women-owned Businesses. *Family Business Review.*

Hisrich, R., Brush, C., Good, D., and DeSouza, G. (1997), Performance in Entrepreneurial Ventures. Does Gender Matter? Frontiers of Entrepreneurship Research. Wellesley, MA: Babson College.

Kamau, D.G., McLean, G.N., and Ardishvili, A. (1999), Perceptions of Business Growth by Women Entrepreneurs. Frontiers of Entrepreneurship Research. Wellesley, MA: Babson College.

Lisowska, E. (1998), Entrepreneurship As A Response to Female Unemployment and Discrimination against Women in the Workplace, Kobieta I Biznes.

Moore, D.P. (2000), Careerpreneurs: Lessons from Leading Women Entrepreneurs on Building A Career without Boundaries. Davies-Black Publishers.

Moore, D.P. and Buttner, H. (1997), Women Entrepreneurs: Moving Beyond the Glass Ceiling. Thousand Oaks, CA: Sage Publications.

Salganicoff, M. (1990), Women in Family Business: Challenges and Opportunities. *Family Business Review.*

Schiller, B.R., and Crewson, P. (1997), Entrepreneurial Origins: A Longitudinal Inquiry. Economic Inquiry.

17

Women Entrepreneurs
SWOT Analysis

C. Venkata Pratyusha

ABSTRACT

Women entreprenurer's have been making a significant impact in all segments of the economy like retail trade, restaurants, hotels, education. Women are active participants in the small and micro-enterprises (SME) sector throughout the world, especially those running informal enterprises. Women sector occupies nearly 45 per cent of the Indian population. However, research has shown that women entrepreneurs face particular socio-cultural, educational and technical constraints to starting, and growing their own enterprises (International Labour Organization, 2003:1). All business owners face certain challenges, but women, because of their gender, often have additional challenges and obstacles that their male peers are less likely to encounter. Indian women have to go a long way to achieve equal rights and position because traditions are deep rooted in Indian society. In addition women entrepreneurs have a number of opportunities which they are not fully taking advantage of such as women associations, conferences and international markets. The purpose of this study is to analyse the Strengths, weakness, opportunities and threats faced by the Women Entrepreneurs.

INTRODUCTION

The Indian sociological set up has been traditionally a male dominated one. Women are considered as weaker sex and always to depend on men folk in their family and outside, throughout their life. They are left with lesser commitments and kept as a dormant force for a quite long time. The Indian culture made them only subordinates and executors of the decisions made by other male members, in the basic family structure. The traditional set up is changing in the modern era. The transformation of social fabric of the Indian society, in terms of increased educational status of women and varied aspirations for better living, necessitated a change in the life style of Indian women. The educated women do not want to limit their lives in the four walls of the house. They demand equal respect from their partners. However, Indian women have to go a long way to achieve equal rights and position because traditions are deep rooted in Indian society. Despite all the social hurdles, many women have become successful in their works. These successful women have made name and wealth for themselves with their hard work, diligence, competence and will power.

WOMEN ENTREPRENEURS

Women's entrepreneurship is both about women's position in society and the role of entrepreneurship in the same society. Indian women are considered as Sakthi, which means source of power, effectively co-ordinating the available factors and resources. Efficient execution of decisions imposed on them clear vision and ambition on the improvement of family and children, patience and bearing the sufferings on behalf of others and ability to work physically more at any age. Women's entrepreneurship needs to be studied for two main reasons. The *first* reason is that women's entrepreneurship has been recognised during the last decade as an important untapped source of economic growth. *Secondly*, the topic of women entrepreneurship has been largely neglected both in society in general and in the social sciences. India is brimming with the success stories of women. They stand tall from the rest of the crowd and are applauded for their achievements in their respective field. These women leaders are assertive, persuasive and willing to take risks. They managed to survive and succeed in this cut throat competition with their hard work, diligence and perseverance. The study of women entrepreneurs reveals new trends. Over the period 1975-95, female self-employment grew by 60 per cent compared to only a 20 per cent increase for men. Recent data from the Centre for Women's Business Research showed that, between 1997 and 2002, women in the United States have formed new businesses at twice the national rate. The Global Entrepreneurship Monitor (GEM) project, a programme of study about entrepreneurs world-wide, has shown a significant amount of female start-up activity around the globe.

OBJECTIVE OF THE STUDY

1. Study role and function of women entrepreneur in the society.
2. Identify the strengths, weakness, opportunities and threats faced by women entrepreneurs on business management in general and entrepreneurship development in particular.

TYPES OF WOMEN ENTREPRENEURS

Women entrepreneurs may be grouped in four broad types. These are: *(i)* Traditional, *(ii)* Innovative; *(iii)* Domestic, and *(iv)* Radical.

- *Traditional:* Women business owners are highly committed to entrepreneurial ideas, as well as to conventional gender roles.
- *Innovative:* Women business owners are highly committed to entrepreneurial ideas but not to traditional gender roles.
- *Domestic:* Women business owners are not committed to entrepreneurial ideas but have a high attachment to entrepreneurial ideas or to traditional gender roles.
- *Radical:* Women business owners have little commitment to entrepreneurial ideas or to traditional gender roles;

these women cannot be seen as entrepreneurial venture seekers. They are usually young, without children and well educated, but have limited work experience (Nieman *et al.* 2006:35).

ROLE OF WOMEN AS AN ENTREPRENEUR'S

1. *Imaginative:* It refers to the imaginative approach or original ideas with competitive market. Well-planned approach is needed to examine the existing situation and to identify the entrepreneurial opportunities. It further implies that women entrepreneur's have association with knowledgeable people and contracting the right organization offering support and services.
2. *Attribute to Work Hard*: Enterprising women have further ability to work hard. The imaginative ideas have to come to a fair play. Hard work is needed to build up an enterprise..
3. *Persistence*: Women entrepreneurs must have an intention to fulfill their dreams. They have to make a dream transferred into an idea enterprise; studies show that successful women work hard.
4. *Ability and Desire to take Risk*: The desire refers to the willingness to take risk and ability to the proficiency in planning making forecast estimates and calculations.
5. *Profit Earning Capacity*: She should have a capacity to get maximum return out of invested capital.

A Woman entrepreneur has also to perform all the functions involved in establishing an enterprise. These include idea generation, and screening, determination of objectives, project preparation, product analysis, determination of forms of business organization, completion of formal activities, raising funds, procuring men machine materials and operations of business.

FUNCTIONS OF A WOMEN ENTREPRENEUR'S

Fredrick Harbiscon, has enumerated the following five functions of a women entrepreneur's:

(i) Exploration of the prospects of starting a new business enterprise.

(ii) Undertaking a risk and handling of economic uncertainties involved in business.

(iii) Introduction of innovations, imitations of innovations.

(iv) Co-ordination, administration and control.

(v) Supervision and leadership.

In nutshell, women entrepreneur are those women who think of a business enterprise, initiate it organize and combine the factors of production, operate the enterprise, undertake risk and handle economic uncertainties involved in running a business enterprise.

There are various motivations for becoming an entrepreneur. There are basically push and pull factors. Push factors are factors that are there due to necessity. Examples are unemployment, insecurity, disagreement with management and lack of alternatives. Pull factors are opportunity driven. One may have a desire for personal development, independence, achievement, recognition and personal wealth. The innovative women entrepreneurs are motivated by limited career progression in large firms. They are ambitious and place a high priority on their businesses.

Female entrepreneurs differ from male entrepreneurs in terms of motivation, business skills, and occupational backgrounds (Hisrich *et al.* 2005:69). A comparison of female and male entrepreneurs is listed in the table below. A significantly large number of women operate as portfolio entrepreneurs, preferring to grow more than one enterprise rather than expanding an existing one. Women entrepreneurs often have a clearly articulated business logic and marketing strategy underpinning their multiple enterprise strategies. In developing countries, a recent survey revealed that the female entrepreneurs from India are generating more wealth than the women in any part of the world. The basic qualities required for entrepreneurs and the basic characters of Indian women, reveal that, much potential is available among the Indian women on their entrepreneurial ability. This potential is to be recognised, brought out and exposed for utilisation in productive and service sectors for the development of the nation.

STRENGTHS OF WOMEN ENTREPRENEURS

1. *Women are Relationship Builders*: Women are cultured to put relationships first. They become masterful relationship builders as a result. In companies where people are working in matrix environments, strong working relationships are critical to success.

Women are more likely to get sub-ordinates to transform their own self-interests into the broader goal the group is trying to achieve. A greater sense of teamwork and commitment to achieving the outcome with others is the result.

2. *Women Connect with Women Buyers*: Research tells us that 50 to 80 per cent of buying decisions are made by women. Yet, many senior level executives are men. Women automatically understand the perspectives of other women and the motivations behind the purchases they make. They know intimately what will be most appealing to female buyers.

This presents a solid business case for having women move up the ranks and lead in senior level roles. It's a competitive advantage to have women leading projects that directly touch the female customer.

3. *Women Intuitively Read Political Dynamics and Emotions*: Women have a well developed ability to read the emotions of people. They have a heightened awareness to subtleties and nuances. Paying attention to this data can help women have the competitive edge because they tap into the feelings of others. This allows them to be ahead of the curve in understanding when people are happy or discontented and why. They also know who to influence and who has the power to get things done.

4. *Women ask Questions*: Women have the courage to ask the seemingly 'dumb' questions. They know that asking questions uncovers the true feelings and perspectives.

They have an ability to ask questions in a way that draws people in and builds trust. The gentle nature that many women naturally have creates an inviting environment of safety and interest. It's easier for employees to speak their point of view when they know it is wanted and valued.

5. *Women A Recollaborative in their Approach*: It is important to women to be inclusive. They know that collaboration is about working together effectively, sharing ideas and information and integrating the best ideas possible.

They work hard to make people feel part of the organization. They appreciate people and let them know their efforts and their work matters. They encourage others to have a say in as many aspects of their work as possible. This could include setting performance goals as well as determining strategy.

WEAKNESS OF WOMEN ENTREPRENEURS

All business owners face certain challenges, but women, because of their gender, often have additional challenges and obstacles that their male peers are less likely to encounter. Working women who have children experience even more demands on time, energy and resources. But this does not mean women are less successful than men, in fact, statistics show that women are starting businesses at more than twice the rate of male-majority-owned businesses. The growing success rate of women entrepreneurs shows that they are resourceful, and able to succeed, despite the odds.

There are three major areas where women business owners may face challenges, less common to men in business:

- Gender Discrimination and Stereotyping.
- Dual Career-family Pressures.
- Lack of Equal Opportunities in Certain Industries.

An ILO study on entrepreneurs in 2002 identified the following challenges faced by women entrepreneurs: *(i)* lack of access to start-up capital, *(ii)* lack of business training/ skills and experience, *(iii)* bureaucratic business registration systems, and *(iv)* negative attitudes by society towards women in business.

Barriers to Women Entrepreneurship

Level Barriers	Individual	Household/ Family	Business	Community/ Government
Financial	Women look for security	Men decide about expenses	Less income= less property= no security= no loan	In some countries, signature of husband required for loan
Economical	Women get less education	Women lack support for household work	Lack of management know-how	Women discriminated in terms of access to economic resources
Socio-cultural	Independent thinking is not allowed to women	Violence against women by husband	Limited mobility – problems with the marketing, transportation and selling of goods	In male dominated industries, women entrepreneurs are not accepted
Political-Legal	Women act privately, not politically	Women have got less influence and negotiation power in the family	Less means to exert power/less protection by the state for women entrepreneurs	Lack of knowledge about women entrepreneurs to be able to develop appropriate policies
Psychological and Philosophical	Low self-esteem, do not dare to demand rights	Women are divided	Women are afraid to be more successful than men/husbands	State views men as the ones who publicly represent the family

The ILO study among many findings found that "76 per cent of women involved in enterprise are in the age category of 20-40. This places heavy reproductive and child care responsibilities on them. These responsibilities are often in competition and conflict with the demands of the women's businesses.

Job discrimination on health grounds is an ethical issue. Velasquez (2004:390) states that "a helpful framework for analysing different forms of discrimination can be constructed by distinguishing the extent to which a discriminatory act is intentional and isolated (or non-instutionalised) and the extent to which it is unintentional and institutionalised". Discrimination in any form is undesirable. Employees should not be discriminated against because they are unwell.

OTHER FACTORS INFLUENCING THE WOMEN ENTREPRENEUR ARE

- *Lack of Confidence* – In general, women lack confidence in their strength and competence. The family members and the society are reluctant to stand beside their entrepreneurial growth. To a certain extent, this situation is changing among Indian women and yet to face a tremendous change to increase the rate of growth in entrepreneurship.
- *Socio-cultural Barriers* – Women's family and personal obligations are sometimes a great barrier for succeeding in business career. Only few women are able to manage both home and business efficiently, devoting enough time to perform all their responsibilities in priority.
- *Market-oriented Risks* – Stiff competition in the market and lack of mobility of women make the dependence of women entrepreneurs on middleman indispensable. Many business women find it difficult to capture the market and make their products popular. They are not fully aware of the changing market conditions and hence can effectively utilise the services of media and internet.
- *Motivational Factors* – Self-motivation can be realized through a mind set for a successful business, attitude to

take up risk and behaviour towards the business society by shouldering the social responsibilities. Other factors are family support, Government policies, financial assistance from public and private institutions and also the environment suitable for women to establish business units.

- *Knowledge in Business Administration* – Women must be educated and trained constantly to acquire the skills and knowledge in all the functional areas of business management. This can facilitate women to excel in decision-making process and develop a good business network.
- *Awareness about the Financial Assistance* – Various institutions in the financial sector extend their maximum support in the form of incentives, loans, schemes etc. Even then every woman entrepreneur may not be aware of all the assistance provided by the institutions. So the sincere efforts taken towards women entrepreneurs may not reach the entrepreneurs in rural and backward areas.
- *Exposed to the Training Programmes* – Training programmes and workshops for every type of entrepreneur is available through the social and welfare associations, based on duration, skill and the purpose of the training programme. Such programmes are really useful to new, rural and young entrepreneurs who want to set up a small and medium scale unit on their own.
- *Identifying the Available Resources* – Women are hesitant to find out the access to cater their needs in the financial and marketing areas. In spite of the mushrooming growth of associations, institutions, and the schemes from the government side, women are not enterprising and dynamic to optimize the resources in the form of reserves, assets mankind or business volunteers.

Specific strategies to help women entrepreneurs succeed include:

- Create a Strong Network.
- Consider Certifying as a Women-owned Business.
- Understand the Power of the Internet.
- Learn New Ways to Balance Work and Life.
- Get Inspiration and Advice From by other Women Succeeding in Business.

Opportunities for Women Entrepreneurs

Highly educated, technically sound and professionally qualified women should be encouraged for managing their own business, rather than dependent on wage employment outlets. The unexplored talents of young women can be identified, trained and used for various types of industries to increase the productivity in the industrial sector. A desirable environment is necessary for every woman to inculcate entrepreneurial values and involve greatly in business dealings. The additional business opportunities that are recently approaching for women entrepreneurs are:

- Eco-friendly technology.
- Bio-technology.
- IT enabled enterprises.
- Event Management.
- Tourism industry.
- Tele-communication.
- Plastic materials.
- Vermiculture.
- Mineral water.
- Sericulture.
- Floriculture.
- Herbal and health care.
- Food, fruits and vegetable processing.

Empowering women entrepreneurs is essential for achieving the goals of sustainable development and the bottlenecks hindering their growth must be eradicated to entitle full participation in the business. Apart from training programmes, Newsletters, mentoring, trade fairs and exhibitions also can be a source for entrepreneurial development. As a result, the desired outcomes of the business are quickly achieved and more of remunerative business opportunities are found. Henceforth, promoting entrepreneurship among women is certainly a short-cut to rapid economic growth and development.

The Citizens Economic Empowerment is another opportunity available to entrepreneurs. The objectives of this reform programme is to unlock the growth potential of citizens through business development support and empowerment initiatives (Ministry of Commerce, Trade and Industry, 2005:38). This programme can be taken advantage of by women entrepreneurs to ensure that they benefit from the funds available for entrepreneurs to develop their businesses.

Other opportunities are in services, agriculture, mining, energy, manufacturing and construction. Service opportunities range from business services (advertising, market research, printing and publishing, consultancy, etc.) communication (tele-communications, courier services) educational services (education and training), health services, transport (air, road, customs and freight forwarding), construction and engineering services, financial services (insurance, banking, asset management), recreational, entertainment and sporting services, energy (generation and transmission of electricity; supply of fuels and lubricants), agriculture, manufacturing and mining (technical services and management consultancy).

It is important for women entrepreneurs to be armed with skills at identifying the right opportunities at the right time. They are a lot of opportunities available to women. The danger lies in women entrepreneurs going for the same or similar opportunities while other profitable opportunities go begging. Banda (2004:2) advises that:

> *"Women entrepreneurship development programmes must cover all aspects not only for establishment and running of enterprises, but also for development of their entrepreneurial and managerial competencies".*

Threats for Women Entrepreneur

Entrepreneur is the key factor of entrepreneurship and now women have been recognised as successful entrepreneurs as they have qualities desirable and relevant for entrepreneurship development. In the process of entrepreneurship, women have to face various problems associated with entrepreneurship and these problems get doubled because of her dual role as a wage earner and a home-maker. According to Reddy (1991) women entrepreneurs feel frustrated at times because they need to spare their time and energy, both towards their business as well as domestic affairs. Women in India constitute a larger proportion of total unemployed population and hence it is imperative to find out the entrepreneurial constraints faced by them. The obstacles women entrepreneurs face are well known, and most of them have experienced the effect of at least one of these challenges:

- Access to Finance.
- Access to Markets.
- Access to Production.
- Access to Information.
- Access to Training.
- Access to and Influence on Policy-makers.

- **Access to Finance**

A prerequisite for starting a firm is to have capital in terms of financial assets and in terms of relevant knowledge assets. Women's position in society has led to a lack of assets in both these aspects. As Finance is a most important aspect of any business. Non-availability of long-term finance, regular and frequent need of working capital and long procedure to avail financial help were found to be the financial problems faced by respondents based on the multiple responses given by them.

- **Access to Markets**

Just as important as access to finance is the challenge of access to markets. In order for a company to be successful, it must be able to sell its products or services. Due to the smaller size of women-controlled businesses, access to markets can pose a very large challenge – in some cases even more difficult than access to finance. During the process of marketing of products women entrepreneurs faced certain problems *viz.*, poor location of shop, lack of transport facility and tough competition from larger and established units.

Often women in business also are not experienced enough to benefit from the trade shows most suitable for their product or service.

- **Access to Production**

Production problems faced by maximum (14%) respondents were non availability of raw-material. According to Kamulun and Kumar (1992) non-availability of raw-material was one of the reasons to the slow growth of women entrepreneurs. Other production problems were non-availability of machine or equipment, lack of training facility and non availability of labour. Major causable factors leading to production problems were high cost of required machine or equipment.

- **Access to Information**

Women-controlled businesses are often small, it is difficult for them to access information they need to expand, learn about innovative programmes available to them or find alternative markets. While technology is being used to assist in delivering information to women-owned businesses, not all businesses have access to such technology. The availability, use of and access to technology differs dramatically. Only a small percentage of women business owners uses technology for anything more sophisticated than word-processing.

- **Access to Training**

Society has traditionally conditioned women to be caregivers, nurturers, and the persons responsible for home and family. In many cases, women's access to training that will assist in developing business skills is limited or difficult to obtain. Because the increase in women business owners has risen dramatically in the last ten years, the number of mentors or role models available to teach other women has not grown as rapidly. Women are also often forced to become the sole providers for their families and therefore are put in a position that they must become entrepreneurs just to exist.

In India, the Association of Women Entrepreneurs of Karnataka, (AWAKE) is trying to address these obstacles by offering free weekly business counseling to women in their local community. Through its local chapters, the Federation of Indian Women Entrepreneurs (FIWE) also helps women entrepreneurs understand the basics of business planning and bank financing – often matching them up with banks that can finance their ventures. Providing this kind of training and education creates the base to build confidence and alleviate poverty.

- **Access to and Influence on Policy-makers**

Governments tend to be male dominated in general, but most especially in the areas of business policy, industry, science, technology, and trade negotiation. There is no question that women have a different approach to policy issues. With the proliferation of multilateral trade agreements, the expansion of multinational corporations into new territories, and the explosion of telecommunications technology, the impact of government policies on small business becomes much more significant. It is absolutely critical that the interests of women business owners are represented in multilateral trade negotiations. The National Association of Women Business Owners (NAWBO) in the United States has developed a highly effective lobbying programme to make policy-makers aware of the concerns of women entrepreneurs.

HOW WOMEN CAN OVER COME THESE TREATS

Women often have life skills and natural abilities that are useful in businesses. Women tend to be great net workers, have inherent skills for negotiating, and the ability to multi-task. Single mothers are often good at delegating and budgeting; skills that they rely on to manage their families.

Specific strategies to help women entrepreneurs succeed include:

- Create a Strong Network.
- Consider Certifying as a Women-owned Business.
- Understand the Power of the Internet.
- Learn New Ways to Balance Work and Life.
- Get Inspiration and Advice From by Other Women Succeeding in Business.

CONCLUSION

Women entrepreneurs have been making a significant impact in all segments of the economy. The areas chosen by women are retail trade, restaurants, hotels, education, cultural, cleaning insurance and manufacturing. A Woman entrepreneur has also to perform all the functions involved in establishing an enterprise. These include idea generation, and screening, determination of objectives etc. Women entrepreneurs face lots of challenges. Women entrepreneurs faced constraints in aspects of financial, marketing production, work place facility and health problems. Business support services, women business associations and organizations need to put in place better measures to effectively address these challenges so as to improve the performance of women enterprises. This paper highlights various strategies of women entrepreneur in the society. Ultimately, female business owners must be recognised for who they are, what they do, and how significantly they impact the world's global economy.

REFERENCES

2003. The Prime Minister's Task Force on Women Entrepreneurs Report and Recommendations. Canada: www.liberal.parl.gc.ca/entrepreneur.

Aldrich, H. (1979), *Organizations and Environments.* Englewoods Cliffs, NJ: Prentice-Hall Inc.

Andrina Lever-Women's Business Organizations: The Hidden Strengths and Potential.

Burt, R. S. (2000), The Network Entrepreneur. In R. Swedberg (Ed.), *Entrepreneurship: The Social Science View*: 281-307. Oxford: England: Oxford University Press.

Colin C Williams, Anjula Gurtoo – Evaluating Indian Women Entrepreneurs in the Informal Sector: Marginalization Dynamics or Rational Economic Choice?

Gabriel Konayuma – Challenges and Opportunities for Zambian Women Entrepreneurs in *Journal of Management and Administration.*

http://www.infibeam.com/Books/info/s-k-dhameja/women-entrepreneurs-opportunities-performance-problems/8176294071.html

http://www.scribd.com/doc/13735212/Women-Entrepreneurs

K. Prakash. Improving Women Entrepreneurs' Competitiveness Through Technology.

Lalitha Iyer: Women Entrepreneurs – Challenges and Strategies Frederic Exert Sifting (FES), New Delhi 1991.

M. Soundarapandian: Women Entrepreneurship – Issues and Strategies. Edited Volume. Kanishka Publishers, New Delhi 1999.

Pooja Nayyar, Avinash Sharma, Jatinder Kishtwaria, Aruna Rana and Neena Vyas J. Soc. Sci., 14(2): 99-102 (2007): Causes and Constraints Faced by Women Entrepreneurs in Entrepreneurial Process.

Rajni Aggarwal, President, Federation of Indian Women Entrepreneurs – Coaching Women Entrepreneurs in India.

Reddi, P.N. (1991), "Problems of Women Entrepreneurs in Goa: A Pilot Study." *Khadi Gramodyog*, 37(4):157-159.

The Monograph '*Gender Issues in Entrepreneurship*' by Maria Minniti, Bobby B. Lyle Chair in Entrepreneurship at SMU's Cox School of Business, is Forthcoming in Foundations and Trends in Entrepreneurship.

Women Entrepreneurship: Issues and Policies by OECD (Organization for Economic Co-operation and Development.)

Women and Leadership: Five Key Strengths Every Organization Needs from HR Management in www.hrmreport.com

18

Women Entrepreneurship
Problems and Prospects

Prof. C. R. R. Reddy*
Dr. U. Prabhakar Reddy**
D. Jayarami Reddy***

Entrepreneurship is a pivotal role in acceleration of industrialization, generation of employment and eradication of poverty and exploitation of natural economic for economic development of a nation. Simply, he translates available economic resources into commercial use. Development of rural India is heavily depends upon industrialization which in turn depends on four 'L's *viz.*, local skill, local resources, local finance and local demand.

The term entrepreneurship, which derived from French word 'entrepreneur', means to undertake. It is an economic activity associated with innovation and creativity, risk and adaptability. Therefore, entrepreneur is an actor, a creator and an innovator who employs certain strategic management practices of profit and growth. Today, entrepreneurship is a password to prosperity, power and fame.

* Former Dean of Commerce and Management and Principal, S.K.U., College Department of Commerce, S. K., University, Anantapur - 515 055, A.P.

** Lecturer in Commerce, Goverment Degree College, Tadipatri, A.P.

*** Lecturer in Commerce, Government Degree College, Anantapur, A.P.

Woman or group of women who initiate, organize and operate a business and is owned and controlled by them having minimum financial interest of 51 per cent of capital and giving at least 51 per cent of employment generated in the enterprise to women is called Women Entrepreneur. Women in business are a recent phenomenon in India; and confine themselves to petty business and tiny cottage industries. Women entrepreneurs engaged in business due to push and pull factors. These factors encourage women to have an independent occupation and stands on their on legs. Women entrepreneurs choose profession as a challenge and urge to do some thing new. Such situation is described as pull factor. Women entrepreneurs are engaged in business activities due to family compulsion and the responsibility thrust upon them is known push factor.

In a way, women entrepreneurship has been recognised during the last decade as an important and untapped source of economic growth.

Not only have women participation at low rate in entrepreneurship than men but they also generally choose to start and manage firms in different industries than men tend to do. The industries (primarily retail, education and other service industries) chosen by women are often perceived as being less important to economic development and growth than high-technology and manufacturing. Mainstream research, policies and programmes tend to be 'men-streamed and too often do not take into account the specific needs of women entrepreneurs. As a consequence, equal opportunity between men and women from the perspective of entrepreneurship is still not a reality. The policy-makers have to address the situation.

Incorporate a women entrepreneurial dimension in considering all small and medium enterprises and growth policies (*e.g.*, meeting women's financing needs at all stages of the business continuum; take-up of business development and support services; access to corporate, government and international markets; technology access and utilisation;

Research and Development and innovation; etc.). Women's entrepreneurship is both about women's position in society and the role of entrepreneurship in the same society. Women are faced with specific obstacles (such as family responsibilities) that have to be overcome in order to give them access to the same opportunities as men.

PROBLEMS OF WOMEN ENTREPRENEURS

Women in India are facing problems in getting ahead of their life in business. A few problems are outlined below:

- The greatest deterrent to women entrepreneurs is that they are women (see note appended). A kind of patriarchal – male dominant social order is the building block to them in their way towards business success.
- The financial institutions are skeptical about the entrepreneurial abilities of women. The bankers consider women loonies as higher risk than men loonies. The bankers put unrealistic and unreasonable securities to get loan to women entrepreneurs. According to a report by the United Nations Industrial Development Organization (UNIDO, 1995), "despite evidence that women's loan repayment rates are higher than men's, women still face more difficulties in obtaining credit," often due to discriminatory attitudes of banks and informal lending groups.
- Entrepreneurs usually require financial assistance of some kind to launch their ventures - be it a formal bank loan or money from a savings account. Women in developing nations have little access to funds, due to the fact that they are concentrated in poor rural communities with few opportunities to borrow money. The women entrepreneurs are suffering from inadequate financial resources and working capital. The women entrepreneurs lack access to external funds due to their inability to provide tangible security. Very few women have the tangible property in hand.
- Women's family obligations also bar them from becoming successful entrepreneurs. Having primary responsibility

for children, home and older dependent family members, few women can devote all their time and energies to their business. The financial institutions discourage women entrepreneurs on the belief that they can at any time leave their business and become housewives again. The result is that they are forced to rely on their own savings, and loan from relatives and family friends.

- Women give more focus to family-ties and relationships. Married women have to make a fine balance between business and home. More over the business success is depend on the support the family members extended to them in the business process and management. The interest of the family members is a determinant factor.
- The male - female competition is another factor, which develop hurdles to women entrepreneurs in the business management process. Despite the fact that Women entrepreneurs are good in keeping their service prompt and delivery in time in spite of lack of organizational skills compared to male entrepreneurs, women have to face constraints from competition. The confidence to travel across day-and-night and even different regions and States are less found in women compared to male entrepreneurs. This shows the low level freedom of expression and freedom of mobility of the women entrepreneurs.
- Knowledge of latest technological changes, know-how, and education level of the person are significant factor that affect business. Women literacy in India is low compared to male population to spur successful entrepreneurship. According to The Economist, this lack of knowledge and the continuing treatment of women as second-class citizens keep them in a pervasive cycle of poverty (The Female Poverty Trap, 2001). Low levels do not provide knowledge of basic accounting as well as self-confidence and self-reliance.
- Low-level risk taking attitude is another factor affecting women – folk decision to get into business. Investing

money, maintaining the operations and retaining profits requires high-risk taking attitude, courage and confidence. Risk tolerance ability of women folk in day-to-day life is high compared to male members, such is not found in business.

- Entrepreneurship capital spans a broad spectrum of social, political, legal, cultural and business values and is shaped by a diverse set of policy instruments, including education, training and taxes. We have seen that the lack of a strong social position for women in combination with a weak general interest in entrepreneurship have a very negative effect on women's entrepreneurship.

DEVELOPING WOMEN ENTREPRENEURS

Increase the ability of women to participate in the labour force by ensuring the availability of affordable child care and equal treatment in the work place. More generally, improving the position of women in society and promoting entrepreneurship generally will have benefits in terms of women's entrepreneurship. Following are suggestions for development of women entrepreneurs.

1. Consider women as a specific target group for all developmental programmes and incorporate a women's entrepreneurial dimension in the formation of all SME-related policies.
2. Extend better educational and training facilities.
3. Extend adequate training on the issues of finance, marketing, production and management skills.
4. Promote the development of women entrepreneur networks which become major sources of knowledge about women's entrepreneurship and valuable tools for its development and promotion.
5. Develop professional competence and leadership skill among women entrepreneurs.
6. The ways with which women involved in this sector in the rural areas are through selling labour (wage labour),

engaging in trading activities (self-employment) and operating small industrial productions (enterprise owners). Working as labour may give them temporary employment but it does not improve their conditions or promote their advancement. Scope of trading activities especially in the rural areas, in view of extensive poverty and the large number of people who need to engage in income earning activities, is limited. Engaging in production or rural industrial activities seems to be the most viable avenue for which the women should be assisted to take up. Non-government organizations have equally need to join hands with the government efforts for economic salvation and provide various forms of opportunities for women to help them earn their living, paving the way for greater entrepreneurship development.

7. Conduct continuous monitoring and improvement of training programmes.
8. Need to extend trade finance by the State finance corporations and financing institutions. Further need to provide more working capital assistance both for small-scale venture and large scale ventures.
9. Women's development corporations have to gain access to open-ended financing.
10. Make provision of micro-credit system and enterprise-credit system to the women entrepreneurs.
11. Infrastructure in the form of industrial plots and sheds to be provided on priority basis.
12. Women Entrepreneurship Development Cell may be formed to appraise problems relating to women enterprises – organization, land, credit, marketing, institutional support including Government.
13. Introduce more governmental schemes motivating women entrepreneurs to engage in small-scale and large-scale business ventures.
14. Involve the Non-governmental Organizations in women entrepreneurial training programmes and counseling.

15. Women entrepreneurs should provide special facilities to develop their enterprises which include:
    (i) advisory services;
    (ii) arrangement of exclusive fairs to promote the products manufactured by women enterprises of small and medium units and quota of stalls for women entrepreneurs at export fairs and Special Economic Zones.

To sum up, Indian independence brought promise of equality of opportunity in all sphere to the Indian women. Unfortunately, the Government sponsored development activities have benefited only a small section of women. A large majority of them are still outside the purview of assistance extended. Suggestions forwarded in this paper will help the entrepreneurs in particular and policy-planners in general to look into this problem, and develop better schemes and create opportunities to the women-folk to enter into a more entrepreneurial venture. Without making any advancement, women will remain a far cry.

NOTE

Gender asymmetry which is a universal phenomenon gives rise to internal and external consequences. The former deal with deprivation of women and the latter is usually neglected and has impact on men and women. Forms gender inequalities are as follows.

- *Mortality Inequality* – Inequality between men and women directly involves the matters of life and death, and takes the brutal form of high mortality rates. It is due to lack of health care and nutrition.
- *Nationality Inequality* – Given situation, prefer boy over girl. It reflects male dominated society inequality can manifest itself in the form of the parents wanting the new born to be a boy rather than a girl.
- *Basic Facility Inequality* – Many countries in the world where girls have less opportunity of schooling than boys do. Even today many women can have less than a square

meal. Afghanistan may be the only country in the world where the government is keen on actively excluding girls from schooling.

- *Special Opportunity Inequality* – Even relative little difference in basic facilities including schooling, the opportunities of higher education may be far fewer for young women than for young men. Indeed gender bias in higher education and professional training can be observed even in some of the richest countries in the world.
- *Professional Inequality* – In employment as well as promotion in work and occupation, women often face grater handicap than men. A country like Japan is quite egalitarian in matters of basic facilities and in higher education and yet progress to elevated levels of employment and occupation seems to be much more problematic for women than men.
- *Ownership Inequality* – Ownership of property of homes and land may be asymmetrically shared. The absence of claims to property can not only reduce the voice of women, but also make it harder for women to enter and flourish in commercial and even social activities. India, in this context did provide equal rights through Legislation.

19

Women Education in India
A Strategic Tool for Development

B. Parimala Devi*
S. D. K. Prathibha**
Dr. G. Rama Krishna***

INDIA AND WOMEN EDUCATION: AN OVERVIEW

India the second highest in terms of population has a share of 17 per cent of the world, but only 2.4 per cent of its land, resulting in tremendous pressures on its natural resources. India is one of the developing countries where males significantly outnumber females, and this has increased over time. Girls and Women education in India plays a vital role in the overall development of the country. It not only helps in the development of human resources, but also improves the quality of life. Educated women not only promote education but also can provide better guidance to their girl child. Moreover educated women can arrest infant mortality rate and growth of the population.

* Assistant Professor, Kottam Tulasi Reddy Engineering College, Kondair, Mahaboob Nagar, A.P.

** Research Scholar in Management, Rayalaseema University, Kurnool, A.P.

*** In-charge, Department of Management, Rayalaseema University, Kurnool, A.P., Email: Drgrkrishna@gmail.com

HISTORY AND GROWTH OF WOMEN EDUCATION IN INDIA

In India, women education started during British rule. During this period, social movements led by eminent personalities and social reformers like Raja Ram Mohan Roy, Kandukuri Veereshalingam Panthulu, Mahatma Jyoti Rao Phoole, Periyar Rama Swamy, Sahoo Maharaj and Baba Saheb Ambedkar emphasized on women's education in India and took various initiatives to make education available to the women of India. Nationalist Government took 22 years to change the education policy of the British rulers. In 1964 the Government of India realized that a change was needed in the education system. Thus an Education Commission was constituted under the chairmanship of Professor D.S. Kothari, which submitted its report in 1966. On the basis of the recommendations submitted by the Education Commission, Government of India announced its National Educational Policy in 1968 enabling free primary education in India. Till 1947, there were only 12 per cent literate Indians. However women's education got an impetus only after the country got independence in 1947 and the government has taken measures to provide education to the women in India. As a result women's literacy rate has grown over the three decades and the growth of female literacy has in fact been higher than that of male literacy rate. In 1971, 22 per cent of Indian women were literates. According to the 1991 census there are 52 per cent literate Indians and by the end of 2001, 54.16 per cent females were literate. The growth of female literacy rate is 14.87 per cent as compared to 11.72 per cent of that of male literacy rate.

In India, girls and women have far less education than men, because of social norms, fears of violence and sexual discrimination. Soon after Indian independence in 1947, making elementary education available to all had become a priority for the Indian government. As discrimination on the basis of caste and gender has been a major impediment in the healthy development of the Indian society, they have been made unlawful by the Indian constitution. The

Parliament has passed the Constitution 86th Amendment Act 2002 to make primary education a fundamental right for children in the age group of 6-14 years. The Scheme of Sarva Shiksha Abhiyan adopted by the Government of India has resolved that all 6-14 age children would complete 8 years of schooling by 2012 and all gender and social category gaps would be bridged at primary education level by 2012. India has the largest population of non-school-going working girls. India being Sovereign, Socialistic, Democratic, Republic, it guarantees free primary education for both boys and girls up to age of 14 years.

This objective has never been fulfilled and primary education in India is not universal. Overall, the literacy rate for women is 53.7 per cent versus 75.3 per cent for men, according to the census report 2001. The breach between rural and urban literacy rate is also very important in India. This is clear from the fact that only 59.4 per cent of rural population are literate as against 80.3 per cent urban population according to the 2001 census. Female literacy rate is lowest in Bihar (33.57%) and highest in Kerala (87.86%). Drop-out rates for girls are very high 53.45 per cent at primary level (I to VIII classes). Eradication of female illiteracy has been one of the major concerns of the government of India since independence. The government organizations and NGOs came out with number of initiatives for the development of women and girls education. The problem is much severe when we analyse the problem by considering religious dimension. According a Survey conducted by ORG-Marg, in 2000-01 in 40 districts of 12 states, almost 60 per cent of the 60 million Muslim women in the country are illiterate with the enrollment percentage of Muslim girl children being a mere 40.66 per cent. As a consequence the proportion of Muslim women in higher education is a mere 3.56 per cent, lower even than that of scheduled castes (4.25 %).

BARRIERS TO GIRLS AND WOMEN EDUCATION

According to a study conducted by Government of India, 41 per cent schools don't have a building, 44 per cent of schools do not have a playground, 54 per cent of schools did not have drinking water, 72 per cent of schools did not have a library, 84 per cent of schools did not have a toilet and 2 per cent of schools had a single teacher. Gender discrimination still persists in India and lot more needs to be done in the field of women's education in India. The gap in the male-female literacy rate is just a simple indicator.

Factors like poverty, presence of a wide child-labour market, absence of assured employment after schooling, Prevailing prejudices, low enrollment of girl child in the schools, engagements of girl children in domestic works and high drop out rate, Parents are hesitant to send their girls to schools that have only male teachers, lack of qualified female teachers is a major barrier to girls' education, problem of access to schools, lack of transport facilities are major obstacles in the path of making all Indian women educated. Fear of sexual harassment is another important aspect in deterring girls from attending schools and a factor contributing to the high drop out rate. Fixed schooling hours do not suit girls in rural areas, as they are needed for domestic work at home or in farms and fields during these hours. This is one of the causes of lower participation rates of girls in education.

WOMEN EDUCATION AND FAMILY PLANNING

Education for girls and women helps in modernizing and revolutionize the ways in thinking of the people. It enlightens them about the need to improve their income sources, saving potential, standard of living and, for this purpose, to restrict the size of their families. Therefore, women education serves as the prime method of family planning and development for better future. Also, as more and more women get education and seek employment, impetus is on for economic development.

Strategies to be Adopted

It has been said popularly that, educating a woman means educating the whole family. In fact, how true it is! Woman has the responsibility of the whole family on herself, an educated woman is better competent of taking care of the health and hygiene. She would educate her children and be a part of social and economic development of the community. Education has a direct impact on women empowerment as they become aware of their rights, their capabilities and get a chance to become independent.

The following strategies are to be adopted to improve girls and women education in India:

- Providing incentives for girl students attending schools,
- Making the learning process more attractive to the children,
- Streamlining the curriculum to make it more vocational and job-oriented,
- Providing better infrastructure,
- Explaining the advantages of sending girls to school
- Making the classroom more child-centered and gender-sensitive,
- Recruiting and training more women teachers, and giving them a regular and living wage,
- Eliminating gender bias from prescribed books,
- Taking special initiatives to serve the most disadvantaged girls,
- Provide bridging education for girls who drop out,
- Supplying safe drinking water and separate toilets for girls,
- Schools within walking distance, closer to the place of dwellings are required etc.

These recommendations can be found in Indian Government policies and some action might have been taken with respect to them. The problem lies in implementation. It is therefore necessary to concentrate on making the system work and deliver the services.

CONCLUSIONS

In spite of all the efforts to develop the primary education system in India, access, equity and quality of elementary education to girls and women in India continue to worry the policy-makers even today. This has been mainly due to the widespread gender discrimination, poverty and various prejudices among the members of the society since ages. The helplessness to check the drop out rates among the girl and women in the rural segments of population is the another cause of worry. However, the renewed emphasis in the education sector in the 11th five-year plan and increased expenditure for primary education can act as palliatives for improving the Indian education system.

REFERENCES

UNICEF, The State of the World's Children, http://www.unicef.org

Long and Arduous Road, http://www.indiatogether.org

http://www.census.gov

NCERT Action Plan, http://ncert.nic.in

www.google.co.in

Index